PSALMS

Worshiping the One True God

John MacArthur

Harper*Christian*
Resources

CONTENTS

INTRODUCTION

Going all the way back to the earliest moments of human history, for as long as there have been interactions between people and God, there has been worship. Indeed, worship has been a critical component of human life and experience for as long as there has been human life and experience. Worship is part of who we are.

This makes sense, of course. When we rightly understand who God is and who we are as fragile, limited beings, the only proper response is worship. When we even begin to contemplate the incredible depths of God's character and power, the only proper response is praise. And when we rightly understand everything God has done on our behalf, the only proper response is thanksgiving expressed through worship. For thousands of years, the book of Psalms has served as the gold standard for worship. Contained within its pages are poignant and powerful expressions of praise, honest and authentic cries from the human heart, artistic expressions of God's character, and much more.

In this study, we will explore many of the Psalms together, sampling the different authors whose offerings of praise are canonized in Scripture. We will learn about the structure and arrangement of the 150 songs and poems that comprise the book of Psalms. And we will engage some of the most famous passages of Scripture ever recorded.

AUTHOR AND DATE

From the divine perspective, the Psalter points to God as its author. But when approaching authorship from the human side, one can identify a collection of more than seven composers. King David wrote at least seventy-three of the 150 Psalms. The sons of Korah accounted for ten (Psalms 42; 44–49; 84; 85; 87). Asaph contributed twelve (Psalms 50; 73–83). Other writers included Solomon (Psalms 72; 127), Moses (Psalm 90), Heman (Psalm 88), and Ethan (Psalm 89). The remaining fifty Psalms remain anonymous in their authorship, though Ezra is thought to be the author of some. The time range in which the Psalms were written in extends from Moses, c. 1410 BC (Psalm 90), to the late sixth or early fifth century BC post-exilic period (Psalm 126), which spans a period of about 900 years of Jewish history.

BACKGROUND AND SETTING

The backdrop for the Psalms is twofold: (1) the acts of God in creation and history, and (2) the history of Israel. Historically, the Psalms range in time from the origin of life to the post-exilic joys of the Jews liberated from Babylon. Thematically, the Psalms cover a wide spectrum of topics ranging from heavenly worship to earthly war. The collected psalms comprise the largest book in the Bible, which is the most frequently quoted Old Testament book in the New Testament. Psalm 117 represents the middle chapter (out of 1,189) in the Bible. Psalm 119 is the largest chapter in the entire Bible. Through the ages, the Psalms have retained their original and primary purpose—to engender the proper praise and worship of God.

HISTORICAL AND THEOLOGICAL THEMES

The basic theme of Psalms is living real life in the real world, where two dimensions operate simultaneously: (1) a *horizontal* or temporal reality, and (2) a *vertical* or transcendent reality. Without denying the pain of the earthly dimension, the people of God are to live joyfully and dependently on the One who stands behind the heavenly/eternal dimension. All cycles of human troubles and triumphs provide occasions for expressing human complaints, confidence, prayers, or praise to Israel's sovereign Lord.

In view of this, the book of Psalms presents a broad array of theology, practically couched in day-to-day reality. The sinfulness of man is documented concretely, not only through the behavioral patterns of the wicked but also by the periodic stumblings of believers. The sovereignty of God is everywhere recognized, but not at the expense of genuine human responsibility. Life often seems to be out of control, and yet all events and situations are understood in the light of divine providence as being right on course according to God's timetable. Assuring glimpses of a future "God's day" bolster the call for perseverance to the end. This book of praise manifests a very practical theology.

A commonly misunderstood phenomenon in Psalms is the association that often develops between the "one" (the psalmist) and the "many" (the theocratic people). Virtually all of the cases of this occur in the psalms of King David. There was an inseparable relationship between the mediatorial ruler and his people; as life went for the king, so it went for the people. Furthermore, at times this union accounted for the psalmist's apparent connection with Christ in the messianic psalms (or messianic portions of certain psalms).

The so-called imprecatory (curse-pronouncing) psalms may be better understood with this perspective. As God's mediatorial representative on earth, David prayed for judgment on his enemies since these enemies were not only hurting him but were primarily hurting God's people. Ultimately, they challenged the King of kings, the God of Israel.

INTERPRETIVE CHALLENGES

It is helpful to recognize certain recurring genres or literary types in the Psalter. Some of the most obvious are: (1) the wisdom type, with instructions for right living; (2) lamentation patterns, which deal with the pangs of life (usually arising from enemies without); (3) penitential psalms (mostly dealing with the "enemy" within, i.e., sin); (4) kingship emphases (universal or mediatorial; theocratic and/ or messianic rule); and (5) thanksgiving psalms. A combination of style and subject matter helps to identify such types when they appear.

The literary characteristic of the Psalms is that all of them are poetry par excellence. Unlike most English poetry, which is based on rhyme and meter, Hebrew poetry is essentially characterized by logical parallelisms. Some of the most important kinds of parallelisms are: (1) *synonymous* (the thought of the first line is restated with similar concepts in the second line, e.g., Psalm 2:1); (2) *antithetic* (the thought of the second line is contrasted with the first, e.g., Psalm 1:6); (3) *climactic* (the second and any subsequent lines pick up a crucial word, phrase, or concept and advance it in a stair-step fashion, e.g., Psalm 29:1–2); and (4) *chiastic* or *introverted* (the logical units are developed in an *A* . . . *B/B* . . . *A* pattern, e.g., Psalm 1:2).

On a larger scale, some psalms in their development from the first to the last verse employ an acrostic or alphabetical arrangement. Psalms 9; 10; 25; 34; 37; 111; 112; 119; and 145 are recognized as either complete or incomplete acrostics. In the Hebrew text, the first letter of the first word of every verse or section begins with a different Hebrew consonant, which advances in alphabetical order until the twenty-two consonants are exhausted. Such a literary vehicle undoubtedly aided in the memorization of the content and served to indicate that its particular subject matter had been covered from "A to Z." Psalm 119 stands out as the most complete example of this device, since the first letter of each of its twenty-two, eight-verse stanzas moves completely through the Hebrew alphabet.

The 150 canonical psalms were organized quite early into five "books." Each of these books ends with a doxology (see Psalms 41:13; 72:18–20; 89:52; 106:48; 150:6). Jewish tradition appealed to the number five and alleged that these divisions echoed the Pentateuch, i.e., the five books of Moses. It is true that there are clusters of psalms, such as (1) those drawn together by an association with an individual or group (e.g., "The sons of Korah," Psalms 42–49; Asaph, Psalms 73–83), (2) those dedicated to a particular function (e.g., "Songs of Ascents," Psalms 120–134), or (3) those devoted explicitly to praise worship (Psalms 146–150). But no one configuration key unlocks the "mystery" as to the organizing theme of this five-book arrangement. Thus, there is no identifiable thematic structure to the entire collection.

1

PSALMS OF WISDOM
Psalms 1–4; 37

DRAWING NEAR
What songs or poems has the Lord used to deepen your understanding of the truth of His Word?

_____

_____

_____

_____

_____

_____

_____

_____

_____

_____

THE CONTEXT
Unlike many of the volumes that we find in the Old Testament, the book of Psalms does not follow one particular historical moment or moments in Israel's history. Instead, the Psalms are part of a literary genre known as *wisdom literature*. This portion of the Old Testament begins with the book of Job and carries through to the book of Ecclesiastes.

In many ways, Psalms serves as a microcosm of the entire Bible. For one thing, it's not a single, continuous book. Instead, Psalms exists as a collection of different writings compiled from several different authors over a period of almost a thousand years. Also, the Psalms contain many different themes and messages that work together to express truth. And while each psalm was written in a specific historical setting through the pen of a human author, each was also inspired by the Holy Spirit to project forward and deliver truth that applied many generations in the future—especially the messianic psalms, which contain specific prophecies about the life and ministry of Christ.

We will begin our exploration of Psalms at the beginning, highlighting the first four of them. Psalms 1 and 2 serve as introductions to the entire book, which reflects an intentional placement. Psalm 3 is a wonderful example of David's ability to turn real-life events—including moments of acute crisis—into opportunities for praise. Psalm 4 is another compact expression of wisdom. And Psalm 37 is similar in both thought and ethos to the Proverbs.

Keys to the Text

Read Psalms 1–4, noting the key words and phrases indicated below.

The Way of the Righteous and the End of the Ungodly: This wisdom psalm functions as an introduction to the entire book of Psalms. Its theme is as big as the whole Bible because it tells of people, paths, and ultimate destinations.

1:1. Blessed: From the perspective of the individual, this is a deep-seated joy and contentment in God; from the perspective of the believing community, it refers to redemptive favor (compare the blessings and cursings of Deuteronomy 27:11–28:6).

The man: By two cycles of contrast, Psalm 1 separates all people into their respective spiritual categories. By observation, all people are separated ethically (verses 1–4); by outcome, all people are separated judicially (verses 5–6).

Walks not . . . nor stands . . . nor sits: The "beatitude" man (see Matthew 5:3–11) is first described as one who avoids such associations as these which exemplify sin's sequential downward drag.

2. His delight . . . in the law: Switching to a positive description, the spiritually "happy" man is characterized by the consistent contemplation and internalization of God's Word for ethical direction and obedience.

3. LIKE A TREE: Because of the mostly arid terrain of Israel, a lush tree served as a fitting symbol of blessing in the Old Testament.

PLANTED: Literally "transplanted." Trees do not plant themselves; neither do sinful people transport themselves into God's kingdom. Salvation is His marvelous work of grace (see Isaiah 61:3; Matthew 15:13). Yet there is genuine responsibility in appropriating the abundant resources of God (see Jeremiah 17:8), which lead to eventual productivity.

4. THE UNGODLY ARE NOT SO: This is an abrupt contrast, literally "not so the wicked!"

CHAFF: A frequent Old Testament word picture from harvest time for what is unsubstantial, without value, and worthy only to be discarded.

5. THEREFORE . . . NOT STAND: "Therefore" introduces the strong conclusion that the ungodly will not be approved by God's judgment.

6. THE LORD KNOWS: This is far more than recognition; the Lord "knows" everything. In this context, the reference is to personal intimacy and involvement with His righteous ones (contrast Matthew 7:23; see 2 Timothy 2:19).

THE WAY OF: The repetition of this phrase picks up on the "path" imagery so characteristic of this psalm. It refers to one's total course of life, i.e., lifestyle. Here, these two courses arrive at the ways of life and death, as in Deuteronomy 30:19; Jeremiah 21:8; see Matthew 7:13–14.

SHALL PERISH: One day the wicked person's way will end in ruin; a new order is coming, and it will be a righteous order. So Psalm 1 begins with the "blessed" and ends with those who "perish" (see Psalms 9:5–6; 112:10).

THE TRIUMPH OF THE KING: Psalm 2 is normally termed "royal" and has had a long history of messianic interpretation. While the function of Psalm 1 is to disclose the two different "ways" that individuals can take—righteousness or unrighteousness—Psalm 2 follows up with its application to nations.

2:1. THE NATIONS: Psalm 2 is said to share with Psalm 1 in the role of introducing the Psalter (see "blessed" in 1:1 and 2:12). Although it has no title, it seems to bear the imprint of David's hand. As such, it fluidly moves from the lesser David through the Davidic dynasty to the greater David—Jesus Christ. Psalm 2 progressively shines its poetic spotlight on four vivid scenes relating to the mutiny of mankind against God: (1) human rebellion (verses 1–3); (2) divine reaction (verses 4–6); (3) divine rule (verses 7–9); (4) human responsibility (verses 10–12).

PLOT A VAIN THING: This is the irony of man's depravity—devising, conspiring, and scheming emptiness (see Psalm 38:12; Proverbs 24:2; Isaiah 59:3, 13).

2. AGAINST . . . AGAINST: The nations and peoples, led by their kings and rulers (see verse 1), direct their hostility toward the Lord and His anointed one. The consecrated and commissioned mediatorial representative referred to David in a near sense and Messiah, i.e., Christ, in the ultimate sense (see Acts 4:25–26).

3. THEIR BONDS . . . THEIR CORDS: Mutinous mankind, instead of understanding that these are God's love-bonds (see Hosea 11:4), views them as yoke-bonds (see Jeremiah 5:5).

5. THEN HE: After mocking them with the laughter of divine contempt, God speaks and acts from His perfectly balanced anger.

6. I HAVE SET MY KING ON MY HOLY HILL: Their puny challenge (see verse 3) is answered by this powerful pronouncement. It is as good as done; His king will be enthroned on Jerusalem's most prominent hill.

7. I WILL DECLARE THE DECREE: The installed mediator now recites the Lord's previously issued enthronement ordinance.

YOU ARE MY SON: This recalls 2 Samuel 7:8–16 as the basis for the Davidic king. It is also the only Old Testament reference to the Father/Son relationship in the Trinity, a relationship decreed in eternity past and demonstrated in the incarnation, thus a major part of the New Testament.

TODAY I HAVE BEGOTTEN YOU: This expresses the privileges of relationship, with its prophetic application to the Son-Messiah. This verse is quoted in the New Testament with reference to the birth of Jesus (see Hebrews 1:5–6) and also to His resurrection (see Acts 13:33–34) as the earthly affirmations.

9. YOU SHALL . . . YOU SHALL: The supreme sovereignty of "the King of kings" is pictured in its subjugating might. The shepherd's "rod" and the king's "scepter" are the same word in the original. Shepherding and kingly imagery often merged in ancient Near Eastern thought (see Micah 7:14).

10–12. NOW THEREFORE: The tone of these verses is surprising. Instead of immediate judgment, the Lord and His Anointed mercifully provide an opportunity for repentance. Five commands place responsibility on mutinous mankind.

12. KISS THE SON: This symbolic act would indicate allegiance and submission (see 1 Samuel 10:1; 1 Kings 19:18). The word for Son here is not the Hebrew

word for son that was used in verse 7, but rather its Aramaic counterpart (see Daniel 7:13), which is a term that would especially be suitable for these commands being addressed to "nations" (verse 1).

PERISH IN THE WAY: These words pick up the major burden of Psalm 1.

THE LORD HELPS HIS PEOPLE: PSALM 3 *intermingles both lament and confidence. In its sweeping scope, it becomes a pattern for praise, peace, and prayer amidst pressure. As it unfolds through three interrelated, historical phenomena, David shares his theological "secret" of having assurance in the face of adversity.*

[A PSALM OF DAVID]: The first of seventy-three psalms attributed to David by superscription. Further information connects its occasion with the Absalom episode (see 2 Samuel 15–18), although many of its features are more descriptive of persecution in general.

3:1–2. INCREASED . . . MANY . . . MANY: The psalmist begins on a low note with his multiplied miseries.

2–3. NO HELP FOR HIM . . . BUT YOU . . . A SHIELD FOR ME: There is a strong contrast between the allegation and the psalmist's assurance. David's attitude and outlook embraces the theology that Paul summarized in Romans 8:31. Psalm 3 also introduces Divine Warrior language (see Exodus 15 as a background).

5. I LAY DOWN AND SLEPT: Since God is known for His sustaining protection, David could relax in the most trying of circumstances.

7. ARISE, O LORD: This is a battle cry for God to engage the enemy and defend His soldiers (see Numbers 10:35; Psalm 68:1).

8. SALVATION BELONGS TO THE LORD: This is a broad-sweeping, all-inclusive deliverance, whether in the temporal or eternal realm.

THE SAFETY OF THE FAITHFUL: *Psalm 4 exhibits the changing attitudes of the worshiper in his most difficult circumstances. David's movement will be from anxiety to assurance as he travels down the road of prayer and trust in God.*

[TO THE CHIEF MUSICIAN]: Psalm 4 introduces the first of fifty-five assignments to the master, director, or chief overseer of worship services in its title.

Further instruction is given in the direction "with stringed instruments." The chief musician, therefore, was to lead the great choir and the string portion of the orchestra in this celebration of worship.

[A PSALM OF DAVID]: There are certain similarities between Psalms 3 and 4. For example, the former is sometimes labeled a morning psalm (see 3:5), while the latter has been called an evening psalm (see 4:8). In both, David is besieged with suffering, injustice, and oppression. Yet at the end of yet another day of pressure, pain, and persecution, David can engage in three conversations which ultimately lead to a point of blessed relaxation: (1) praying to God for preservation (verse 1); (2) reasoning with his enemies about repentance (verses 2–5); and (3) praising God for true perspective (verses 6–8).

4:1. O GOD OF MY RIGHTEOUSNESS: The ultimate basis for divine intervention resides in God, not in the psalmist. For insight about union with God's righteousness based on His mercy, see Jeremiah 23:6 (see also 1 Corinthians 1:30).

DISTRESS: This is an important word for trying circumstances in the Psalms. It pictures the psalmist's plight as being in straits, i.e., painfully restricted. Here, his testimony to God's historical salvation, "you have relieved me," conveys the picture that his Lord had provided space or room for him.

2–3. HOW LONG ... HOW LONG: God's agenda for David (verse 3) is radically contrasted with that of his enemies (verse 2). The term for "godly" or pious in the Old Testament is above all else indicating a person blessed by God's grace.

4. BE ANGRY, AND DO NOT SIN: The admonition means to tremble or shake in the fear of the Lord so as not to sin (see Isaiah 32:10–11; Habakkuk 3:16).

5. TRUST: This command reflects the primary word group in the Old Testament for faith-commitment.

6–8. THERE ARE MANY WHO SAY: The taunting skeptics are cut off by the testimony of the psalmist's rest because of God's personal blessings.

8. DWELL IN SAFETY: The word "safety" introduces a play on words by going back to the term "trust" in verse 5. David evidences a total confidence in God in the midst of his crisis.

Read Psalm 37, noting the key words and phrases indicated below.

THE HERITAGE OF THE RIGHTEOUS AND THE CALAMITY OF THE WICKED: The basic theme of Psalm 37 deals with the age-old question,

"Why do the ungodly prosper, while the godly painfully struggle through life?" An intricate arrangement puts forth David's answer.

37:1. DO NOT FRET BECAUSE OF EVILDOERS: Psalm 37, an irregular acrostic, is a wisdom poem addressed to man, not God. Verses 12–24 sound very much like the maxims of Proverbs. The covenant promises of the "land" for Israel are prominent in its verses (see 3, 9, 11, 22, 29, 34). David mixes and matches six thoughts in order to advance his major message on the eventual arrival of divine justice: (1) an introductory overview (verses 1–2); (2) an initial expansion (verses 3–11); (3) some proverbial perspectives (verses 12–24); (4) an initial testimony (verses 25–26); (5) a final expansion (verses 27–34; see also verses 3–11); and (6) a final testimony (verses 35–40; see also verses 25–26).

2. BE CUT DOWN: Here-today, gone-tomorrow illustrations about the wicked characterize this psalm. On this theme, see Job 14:1, 2; Psalms 90:5–6; 103:15–16; Isaiah 40:6–8; Matthew 6:30; James 1:10–11; 1 John 2:17.

7–8. DO NOT FRET: The message of "Relax! Don't react!" returns (see verse 1).

10. YET A LITTLE WHILE: See similar terminology used in Jeremiah 51:33 and Hosea 1:4. The Lord's intervention is imminent.

17. THE ARMS OF THE WICKED SHALL BE BROKEN: Their members will be shattered for illicitly grabbing their wealth (see verse 16b). See also Job 38:15; Psalm 10:15; Jeremiah 48:25; Ezekiel 30:21.

21. THE WICKED BORROWS: The Old Testament contains both precepts and proverbs about borrowing and lending. See Deuteronomy 15:6; 28:12, 44; Psalm 112:16; Proverbs 22:7.

24. HE SHALL NOT BE UTTERLY CAST DOWN: For corroborations of such divine comfort, see Psalm 145:14; Proverbs 24:16; Micah 7:8.

31. THE LAW OF HIS GOD IS IN HIS HEART: On God's internalized instruction, see Deuteronomy 6:6; Psalms 40:8; 119 (throughout); Jeremiah 31:33; Isaiah 51:7.

38. CUT OFF: On this truth of judgment, see verses 9, 22, 28, 34, and Psalm 109:13. For a positive presentation in reference to the faithful, see Proverbs 23:18; 24:14, 20.

39. SALVATION . . . FROM THE LORD: Since salvation belongs to Him (see Psalm 3:8), He is the perennial Source of it (see Psalm 62:1–2).

UNLEASHING THE TEXT

1) What are the key images in Psalm 1, and what does each communicate?

_____

_____

_____

_____

_____

2) What specific aspects of God's character are communicated in Psalm 2?

_____

_____

_____

_____

3) How should we understand the concept of "salvation" expressed in Psalm 3?

_____

_____

_____

_____

_____

4) What is the primary message of Psalm 37?

_____

_____

_____

_____

_____

EXPLORING THE MEANING

We can choose blessing. One of the core themes repeated in the Bible is that God's people have been offered a choice. They can choose to live in obedient submission to God and receive blessing, or they can choose to live in rebellion against God and receive curses. This choice was pictured at the very beginning of God's Word when Adam and Eve were placed in the Garden of Eden and given that choice: Obey God and live; disobey and die. Psalm 1 introduces the entire collection of psalms by once again presenting the reader with that choice. In this case, the psalmist offers a stark comparison between those who choose righteousness and those who choose wickedness. First and foremost, those who choose righteousness will be "blessed" (Psalm 1:1)—a word that is rich in depth and promise. Also, the righteous will be like trees "planted by the rivers of water" (verse 3), which bear much fruit. The wicked, however, will be "like the chaff which the wind drives away" (verse 4).

The righteous serve the true King: While Psalm 1 is a personal reflection about righteousness and rebellion, Psalm 2 carries those themes to a broader audience: the nations and civilizations. The choice presented is the same as in Psalm 1—choose service to God and be blessed, or choose rebellion against God and face His wrath. The contrasts built into the psalm are as powerful as they are stark. On one hand, the "nations rage," the "people plot," and "the kings of the earth set themselves . . . against the LORD and against His Anointed" (Psalm 2: 1–2). The picture being painted is of rulers and armies stirring themselves up in rebellion against God. In response, "He who sits in the heavens shall laugh; The LORD shall hold them in derision. Then He shall speak to them in His wrath, And distress them in His deep displeasure" (verses 4–5). The psalm ends with a call for those who consider themselves powerful to submit to the only Being in creation who truly carries authority: "Be wise, O kings. . . . Serve the LORD with fear, and rejoice with trembling. Kiss the Son, lest He be angry, and you perish in the way, when His wrath is kindled but a little. Blessed are those who put their trust in Him" (verses 10–12).

Pursuing righteousness does not preclude individual aspirations. Submitting to the will of God does not necessarily mean that we give up personal desires. We should never pursue anything that is opposed to God and His righteous character, but we are free to enjoy whatever is not immoral. Nevertheless, we are called to submit everything we do to the will of God, seeking to honor Him in everything. If you "delight yourself also in the LORD," then "He shall give you the desires of your heart" (Psalm 37:4). But notice that "delight[ing] . . . in the LORD" is the condition He demands before you receive "the desires of your heart." This means that whatever you desire is in accordance with God's character, or at least not contrary to it. Therefore, you are free to pursue your own heart's desires so long as those desires do not violate God's law. Ecclesiastes 11:9 reads, "Rejoice, young man, during your childhood, and let your heart be pleasant during the days of young manhood. And follow the impulses of your heart and the desires of your eyes. Yet know that God will bring you to judgment for all these things" (NASB).

REFLECTING ON THE TEXT

5) List out and rehearse to yourself specific blessings you've received from the Lord in the past.

_____

_____

_____

_____

_____

_____

6) Recall an important moment of choosing between serving God and rebelling against Him. Assess spiritually, based on these opening Psalms, what happened.

_____

_____

_____

_____

_____

_____

7) Where do you see nations and peoples still setting themselves against God and rebelling against His will? Where do you see yourself failing in the same ways?

_____

_____

_____

_____

_____

8) What "desires of your heart" are you seeking, and why are they important to you? What other scriptures show you whether those desires glorify God or not? Examine each one carefully.

_____

_____

_____

_____

_____

_____

PERSONAL RESPONSE

9) Bring to God the heart desires you just examined. Ask Him to help conform them to His own, as He's shown them to us in Scripture. What are you doing well? What do you need to change?

_____

_____

_____

_____

_____

_____

10) Whom else are you helping to understand the choice between serving God and serving self? How are you doing with it yourself?

_____

_____

_____

_____

_____

_____

2

PSALMS OF COMFORT

Psalms 16; 19–21; 23; 27

DRAWING NEAR

Where do you tend to turn when you are looking for comfort? Why that particular source?

_____

_____

_____

_____

_____

_____

_____

_____

_____

_____

_____

THE CONTEXT

We saw in the previous lesson that many of the Psalms were written as artistic expressions of wisdom. For instance, Psalm 1 provides wisdom to readers on the blessings that are associated with pursuing righteousness (verses 1–3), contrasted with the dire consequences that await those who choose the path of the ungodly (verses 4–6). Such psalms often center around a single key theme and offer a condensed and poignant reflection on truth.

In this lesson, we will take a look at several psalms that were written to offer comfort to those who read or sang them. Some of these psalms are connected to specific events or circumstances, such as Psalm 20 and 21, which directly address God's people before and after a battle. Other psalms in this group are more general in offering comfort based on God's character. Psalm 23, for example, is perhaps the most famous passage of the Old Testament because it is a compact, visual, and beautiful expression of God's goodness even in the face of difficult circumstances.

Each of the psalms in this section were written by King David, who is the most famous and most prolific author within the Psalter. David is directly named as the author of seventy-three psalms (out of a total of 150); however, the New Testament attributes David to be the author of two more: Psalm 2 (see Acts 4:25) and Psalm 95 (see Hebrews 4:7).

KEYS TO THE TEXT

Read Psalm 16, noting the key words and phrases indicated below.

THE HOPE OF THE FAITHFUL, AND THE MESSIAH'S VICTORY: The only prayer of Psalm 16 comes in the first line: "Preserve me, O God" (verse 1). The rest of the psalm consists of David's weaving together his personal testimonies of trust in the Lord.

[A MICHTAM OF DAVID]: For similar designations, see Psalms 56; 57; 58; 59; 60. In spite of many conjectures, this designation remains obscure.

16:1. PRESERVE ME: This is a frequent request, begging God to protect the psalmist (see Psalms 17:8; 140:4; 141:9).

IN YOU I PUT MY TRUST: This opening prayer from David is bolstered in the rest of the psalm by two cycles of testimony: (1) his testimony of communion, including its divine and human dimensions (verses 2–4); and (2) his testimony of confidence, including its past and present dimensions (verses 5–8), and its present and future dimensions (verses 9–11).

2. O MY SOUL, YOU HAVE SAID: The italicized words indicate there is a variant in the Hebrew Bible concerning the verb. It may be just as well to regard the verb as a shortened form of "I said" (also occurring at 1 Kings 8:48; Job 42:2; Psalm 140:13; Ezekiel 16:59).

MY GOODNESS IS NOTHING APART FROM YOU: In other words, "My well-being is entirely dependent on You."

4. THEIR SORROWS SHALL BE MULTIPLIED: The psalmist will have nothing to do with false gods or the people pursuing them.

5–6. MY INHERITANCE . . . MY CUP . . . MY LOT . . . THE LINES . . . PLEASANT PLACES: These lines use Old Testament metaphors to describe the blessings of God.

9. MY GLORY: Starting back at verse 7, the psalmist referred to his core of being as literally "my kidneys," then "my heart," now "my glory," and next "my flesh" and "my soul." The anthropological terms stand for the whole person; so, it is best to consider "my glory" as referring to that distinctive way in which man is created in the image of God, i.e., his intelligence and ability to speak.

10. YOU WILL NOT LEAVE MY SOUL IN SHEOL: These words expressed the confidence of the lesser David, but were applied messianically to the resurrection of the greater David (the Lord Jesus Christ), both by Peter (see Acts 2:25–28) and Paul (see Acts 13:35).

Read Psalms 19–21, noting the key words and phrases indicated below.

> THE PERFECT REVELATION OF THE LORD: In Psalm 19, David
> depicts the LORD God as author of both His world and His Word
> in this unified hymn. He shows how God has revealed Himself
> to mankind through these two avenues.

19:1. THE HEAVENS . . . THE FIRMAMENT: Both are crucial elements in God's creation of the world (see Genesis 1:1–8).

DECLARE . . . SHOWS: Both verbs emphasize the continuity of these respective disclosures.

HIS HANDIWORK: An anthropomorphism illustrating God's great power (see the "work of His fingers" in Psalm 8:3). The human race stands accountable to God because of His nonverbal and verbal communications. In light of these intentions, Psalm 19 summarizes two prominent avenues of God's self-disclosure: (1) God's general self-disclosure in the world, including his publication of the skies (verses 1–4b) and the prominence of the sun (verses 4c–6); and (2) God's special self-disclosure in the Word, including the attributes of the

Word (verses 7–9), an appreciation for the Word (verses 10–11), and the application of the Word (verses 12–14).

GLORY OF GOD: Because of this psalm's two distinct parts and two different names for God, some have tried to argue that Psalm 19 was really two compositions, one ancient and one more recent. However, the shorter form of the name "God" speaks of His power, especially His power exhibited as Creator, while the name "LORD" fits the relational focus.

2–6. DAY UNTO DAY: The testimony of the universe comes forth consistently and clearly, but sinful mankind persistently resists it. For this reason, general revelation cannot convert sinners, but it does make them highly accountable (see Romans 1:18ff.). Salvation ultimately comes through special revelation alone, i.e., as the Word of God is effectually applied by the Spirit of God.

2–3. SPEECH . . . NO SPEECH: This is not a contradiction, but shows that the constant communication of the heavens is not with words of a literal nature.

4. THEIR LINE HAS GONE OUT: The message of the created world extends to everywhere.

4C–6. TABERNACLE FOR THE SUN . . . HEAVEN: Neither the sun nor the heavens are deified as was the case in many pagan religions. In the Bible, God is the creator and ruler over all creation.

7–9. LAW . . . TESTIMONY . . . STATUTES . . . COMMANDMENT . . . FEAR . . . JUDGMENTS: The scene here shifts from God's world to God's Word. This section contains six names for God's Word, followed appropriately by six characteristics and six achievements. Each of the four parallel lines contains a word (a synonym) for God's Word; each describes what His Word is; and each pronounces what it effectually accomplishes.

7. LAW: This might be better translated, "His teaching," "a direction," or "instruction" (see Psalm 1:2).

TESTIMONY: This word for the Word derives from the root "to bear witness." It, so to speak, bears testimony to its divine author.

8. STATUTES: This synonym looks upon God's Word as orders, charges, and precepts. They are viewed as the governor's governings.

COMMANDMENT: This word is related to the verb "to command" or "to order." The Word is, therefore, also perceived as divine orders.

9. FEAR: This is not technically a word for the Word, but it does reflect the reality that Scripture is the manual for worship of God.

JUDGMENTS: This term looks upon God's Word as conveying His judicial decisions.

12–13. WHO CAN UNDERSTAND HIS ERRORS? The psalmist deals respectively with unintentional sins and high-handed infractions (see Leviticus 4:1ff.; Numbers 15:22ff.). David's concerns reflect the attitude of a maturing disciple who, by God's grace and provisions, deals with his sins and does not deny them.

14. BE ACCEPTABLE: Using a term often associated with God's acceptance of properly offered, literal sacrifices, David asks for grace and enablement as he lays his "lip-and-life" sacrifices on the "altar" (see Joshua 1:8).

THE ASSURANCE OF GOD'S SAVING WORK: Psalms 20 and 21, both written by King David, are twin warfare events. Psalm 20 is mostly ceremony before a battle, while Psalm 21 is mostly celebration after a battle.

20:1. MAY THE LORD ANSWER YOU: This is the prayer of God's people for their king-general (see "His anointed," verse 6). In a theocracy, battles were to be considered holy wars. The chain of command was (1) the Lord as commander-in-chief over (2) the anointed king-general and (3) the theocratic people—soldiers. All holy convocations, both before and after battles, involved prayer and praise assemblies dedicated to God, who grants victories through the theocratic king-general. Psalm 20, in anticipation of a military campaign, commemorates a three-phased ceremony regularly conducted by the people in the presence of the commander-in-chief on behalf of the king-general: (1) an offering of their prayers (verses 1–5); (2) a confirmation of their confidence (verses 6–8); and (3) a reaffirmation of their dependence (verse 9).

2. FROM THE SANCTUARY . . . OUT OF ZION: These are designations about the place of God's symbolic presence in the ark, which David had recaptured and installed in a tabernacle on Mount Zion. The people's wish was that the Lord Himself would uphold, support, and sustain the king-general with His extending, powerful presence throughout the military campaign.

5. YOUR SALVATION: Here, by contrast, God's salvation is victory in battle.

7. SOME TRUST IN: Trust, boast, and praise must not be directed to the wrong objects but only to God Himself (see, e.g., Deuteronomy 17:16; 20:1–4; Leviticus 26:7–8; Psalm 33:16–17; Isaiah 31:1–3; Jeremiah 9:23–24; Zechariah 4:6).

9. SAVE, LORD! This verse could also be rendered: "LORD, grant victory to the king! Answer us when we call!"

JOY IN THE SALVATION OF THE LORD: Psalm 21, as previously noted, is mostly celebration after a battle. The first part is a thanksgiving for victory; the last part is an anticipation of future victories in the Lord through the king-general.

21:1. THE KING SHALL HAVE JOY: Two scenarios of victory provide a context for praise and prayer to the commander-in-chief (the Lord) of Israel's king-general: (1) a present-past scenario of praise, grounded in victories accomplished in the Lord (verses 1–6); and (2) a present-future scenario of prayer and praise: grounded in victories anticipated in the Lord (verses 7–13).

2. YOU HAVE GIVEN HIM HIS HEART'S DESIRE: The "before" part of this statement is found in Psalm 20:4: "May He grant you according to your heart's desire."

3. YOU SET A CROWN OF PURE GOLD UPON HIS HEAD: This is symbolic of superlative blessing (note the reversal in Ezekiel 21:25–27).

4. HE ASKED LIFE FROM YOU ... LENGTH OF DAYS: The first part of the verse most likely pertains to preservation of life in battle, and the second part to perpetuation of the dynasty (see 2 Samuel 7:13, 16, 29; Psalm 89:4; 132:12).

5–6. GREAT IN YOUR SALVATION: The King had given great prominence to the king-general.

7. FOR THE KING: The human responsibility dimension of the previous divine blessings is identified as the king-general's dependent trust in God. But the sovereign grace of God provides the ultimate basis for one not being "moved" or shaken (see Psalms 15:5; 16:8; 17:5; Proverbs 10:30).

8. YOUR HAND ... HATE YOU: Without denying the mediatorship of the king-general, these delineations obviously put the spotlight upon the commander-in-chief (God).

Read Psalm 23, noting the key words and phrases indicated below.

THE LORD, THE SHEPHERD OF HIS PEOPLE: Psalm 23, probably the best-known passage in the Old Testament, is a testimony by David

to the Lord's faithfulness in his life. As a hymn of confidence,
it pictures the Lord as a disciple's Shepherd-King-Host.

23:1. THE LORD: David uses common ancient Near Eastern images in this psalm to progressively unveil his personal relationship with the Lord in three stages: (1) his exclamation: "The Lord is my shepherd" (verse 1a); (2) his expectations: "I shall not want" (verse 1b–3), and "I will fear no evil" (verses 4–5b); and (3) his exultation: "my cup runs over" (verse 5c–6).

MY SHEPHERD: On the image of the Lord as a shepherd, see Genesis 48:15; 49:24; Deuteronomy 32:6–12; Psalms 28:9; 74:1; 77:20; 78:52; 79:13; 80:1; 95:7; 100:3; Isaiah 40:11; Jeremiah 23:3; Ezekiel 34; Hosea 4:16; Micah 5:4; 7:14; and Zechariah 9:16. This imagery was used commonly in kingly applications and is frequently applied to Jesus in the New Testament (see, e.g., John 10; Hebrews 13:20; 1 Peter 2:25; 5:4).

2–3. MAKES ME LIE DOWN . . . LEADS ME . . . RESTORES MY SOUL . . . LEADS ME: These four characterizing activities of the Lord as shepherd (i.e., emphasizing His grace and guidance) are followed by the ultimate basis for His goodness, i.e., "His name's sake" (see Psalms 25:11; 31:3; 106:8; Isaiah 43:25; 48:9; Ezekiel 36:22–32).

4. THE VALLEY OF THE SHADOW OF DEATH: Phraseology used to convey a perilously threatening environment (see Job 10:21, 22; 38:17; Psalms 44:19; 107:10; Jeremiah 2:6; Luke 1:79).

YOUR ROD AND YOUR STAFF, THEY COMFORT ME: The shepherd's club and crook are viewed as comforting instruments of protection and direction, respectively.

5. YOU PREPARE A TABLE: The able protector (see verse 4) is also the abundant provider.

YOU ANOINT MY HEAD: The biblical imagery of anointing is frequently associated with blessing (see Psalms 45:7; 92:10; 104:15; 133:2; Ecclesiastes 9:8; Amos 6:6; Luke 7:46).

6. AND I WILL DWELL IN THE HOUSE OF THE LORD FOREVER: There is some question concerning the form in the Hebrew text (see also Psalm 27:4). Should it be rendered "I shall return" or "I shall dwell"? Whichever way it is taken, by the grace of his Lord, David is expecting ongoing opportunities of intimate fellowship.

Read Psalm 27, noting the key words and phrases indicated below.

A DECLARATION OF FAITH: Psalm 27 is characterized by strong contrasts such as lament and laud; persecution and praise; plus warfare and worship.

27:1. THE LORD IS: The psalmist, in the presence of his Lord, engages in three conversations that help him balance the ups and downs of life: (1) he converses with himself about privileges (verses 1–6); (2) he converses with the Lord about problems (verses 7–12); (3) he converses with himself about perseverance (verses 13–14).

LIGHT: This important biblical word picture with exclusively positive connotations pictures the light of redemption in contrast to the darkness of condemnation (see Psalms 18:28; 36:9; 43:3; Isaiah 60:1, 19, 20; Micah 7:8; John 8:12; 12:46; 1 John 1:5).

2. TO EAT UP MY FLESH: An allusion to the psalmist's enemies being like vicious beasts (see Psalms 7:2; 14:4; 17:12; Job 19:22; Jeremiah 30:16; 50:7). This wording was also employed to describe slander and defamation (see a close Aramaic parallel in Daniel 3:8; 6:24).

THEY STUMBLED AND FELL: This doublet conveys thorough defeat (see Isaiah 3:8; 8:15; 31:3; Jeremiah 46:6).

4. ONE THING I HAVE DESIRED: The primary issue in David's life was to live in God's presence and by His purpose (see Psalms 15:1; 23:6; see also Paul's "one thing" in Philippians 3:13).

5. HIS PAVILION: David portrays the privileges of divine protection as being hidden in God's "booth" or "shelter," a term in parallelism with "tabernacle" or "tent."

8–9. SEEK MY FACE . . . YOUR FACE . . . YOUR FACE: God's "face" indicates His personal presence or simply His being (see Psalms 24:6; 105:4); and seeking His face is a primary characteristic of true believers who desire fellowship with Him (see Deuteronomy 4:29; 2 Chronicles 11:16; 20:4; Psalm 40:16; Jeremiah 50:4; Hosea 3:5; Zechariah 8:22).

10. MY FATHER AND MY MOTHER FORSAKE ME: Even though those nearest and dearest to David might abandon him, his Lord would always be concerned about and care for him (see Deuteronomy 31:6, 8; Isaiah 49:14, 15; Hebrews 13:5).

14. WAIT . . . WAIT: This particular word for waiting connotes either a tense or eager and patient anticipation of the Lord (see Psalms 37:34; 40:1).

UNLEASHING THE TEXT

1) What does Psalm 19 teach about God's Word?

_____

_____

_____

_____

2) Examine the differences between how Psalms 20 and 21 use the word *king* and list some of those differences below.

_____

_____

_____

_____

_____

3) Psalm 23 is a familiar passage, but reread it carefully. What main point is David expressing?

_____

_____

_____

_____

4) How does Psalm 27 address the idea of comfort?

_____

_____

_____

_____

EXPLORING THE MEANING

We can find comfort in God's Word. Psalm 19 begins with wonderful expressions of praise to God, with David connecting different aspects of creation to the glorious nature of God's character. The second half of the psalm shifts away from the world and focuses squarely on God's Word: "The law of the LORD is perfect, converting the soul; the testimony of the LORD is sure, making wise the simple; the statutes of the LORD are right, rejoicing the heart; the commandment of the LORD is pure, enlightening the eyes" (verses 7–8). These are beautiful expressions of admiration and adoration from David for the Scriptures—both for what they themselves are, and for what they accomplish in our lives. The Bible is more desirable than gold, "Yea, than much fine gold," and, "Sweeter also than honey and the honeycomb" (verse 10). The incredible value of God's Word should not be lost on modern readers who, unlike David, have access to the full canon of Scripture. That value can be an amazing source of comfort. No matter what happens in life—no matter what we endure or what we might face—we have access to the very words of God spoken to bless and benefit us.

We can find comfort in God's strength. Not only do we have access to the Bible to bring us comfort during difficult times, but we also have access to the Author of the Scriptures, God Himself. Psalm 20 was written as a ceremonial blessing before battle—specifically, a blessing for the king among God's people. As the king himself, David knew where to go when he was in need of both comfort and strength: "Some trust in chariots, and some in horses; but we will remember the name of the LORD our God" (verse 7). Psalm 21 was written as a celebration of a victorious battle. Once again, David made certain to identify the real Source of any victory: "The king shall have joy in Your strength, O LORD; and in Your salvation how greatly shall he rejoice!" (verse 1). David ended with a sentiment we can (and should) echo today: "Be exalted, O LORD, in Your own strength! We will sing and praise Your power" (verse 13). Even as we worship God for His incredible strength, we can find comfort that He uses that strength on our behalf.

We can find comfort in God's direction. There is an interesting detail in Psalm 23 that is often overlooked: "Yea, though I walk through the valley of the shadow of death, I will fear no evil; for You are with me; Your rod and Your staff, they comfort me" (verse 4) We see the value of God's presence when we are within "the valley of the shadow of death." But what about God's "rod" and "staff"? How do those instruments provide "comfort"? In the ancient world, shepherds used several tools to carry out their duties. The rod and staff, sometimes called the club and crook, each had a function. The former was for protection. If the sheep were under attack, the shepherd could strike the antagonists with the club and drive them off. The staff was typically a tall pole with a curve at the end. If a sheep wandered off in the wrong direction, the shepherd could "hook" the end of the staff around its neck and pull it back into line. Of course, even the most dedicated followers of Jesus will at times go astray. It's comforting, therefore, to know that Christ Himself, the Good Shepherd, is watching. Not only is he watching, but He provides direction and even re-direction when we need it.

REFLECTING ON THE TEXT

5) What do passages like Psalms 19, 20, and 23 reflect about God's character?

_____

_____

_____

_____

_____

_____

_____

6) How do these aspects of God's character bring you comfort?

_____

_____

_____

_____

_____

_____

7) What are some examples of God displaying His strength in Psalms 20 and 21? Does this stir you to worship Him? Explain your answer.

_____

_____

_____

_____

_____

8) What is the appropriate response to God's leading or directing us toward a specific path?

_____

_____

_____

_____

_____

PERSONAL RESPONSE

9) Why are Christians in need of comfort? Think of specific people you know. How can you be more aware of your need of God and express that reality to others?

_____

_____

_____

_____

_____

10) Every aspect of your life needs to be subjected to God's direction. So how do these Psalms show you to seek that direction from God?

_____

_____

_____

_____

_____

3

PSALMS OF REPENTANCE

Psalms 30–32; 38–39; 51

DRAWING NEAR

Confession and repentance are necessary and vital aspects of the Christian life. Do you frequently confess your sin to God and repent of it?

_____

_____

_____

_____

_____

_____

_____

_____

_____

THE CONTEXT

The first lesson of this study focused on psalms centered on the theme of wisdom, and the second lesson focused on psalms rooted in the theme of compassion. As noted previously, each of the psalms explored in lesson 2 were written by David, and we will continue to explore David's work in this lesson as we study psalms that lift up the theme of repentance.

David's public adultery with Bathsheba is perhaps the most infamous episode in his life. David already had several wives, but he used his authority as the king of Israel to sleep with Bathsheba, who was also married. When Bathsheba conceived, David attempted to cover up his sin by sending for her husband, Uriah, who was one of his soldiers away at war for Israel. When this cover-up failed, David arranged for Uriah to be killed in battle. David then took Bathsheba as another of his wives. But the Lord used Nathan the prophet to expose all of these machinations (see 2 Samuel 11–12).

In this lesson we will explore Psalm 51, which was a deeply personal and emotional confession written by King David after the Lord exposed his sin with Bathsheba. Psalm 32 is also believed to be connected with that incident. Having confessed his sin, David reflects on the joy of forgiveness. The remainder of the psalms explored in this section also touch on those critical themes.

Keys to the Text

Read Psalms 30–32, noting the key words and phrases indicated below.

> THE BLESSEDNESS OF ANSWERED PRAYER: *A mixture of forms characterize David's words in Psalm 30. The Israelite king speaks out of a cycle of life (lamentation and laud), especially moving through prayer to praise.*

[A PSALM. A SONG AT THE DEDICATION OF THE HOUSE OF DAVID]: The first and last parts of this title, "A Psalm . . . of David," are common notations in the superscriptions of many psalms. However, the middle words, "a song of dedication," or "consecration of the house," were probably added later, though they could have referenced David's temporary tent representative of the ark erected on Mt. Zion (see 2 Samuel 6:17) or his own house (see 2 Samuel 5:11–12).

30:1. I WILL EXTOL YOU, O LORD: In spite of the great variety of forms found in this psalm, it is bonded together by praise emphases (see verses 4, 9, 12). David's beginning and ending pledges to praise provide structure for his prayers and testimonies: (1) his beginning pledge of praise (verse 1a); (2) his look back on historic prayers and testimonies (verses 1b–9); (3) his look ahead to continuing prayers and testimonies (verses 10–12a); and (4) his concluding pledge of praise (verse 12b).

2–3. YOU HEALED ME: God alone is the unique healer (see Exodus 15:26; Deuteronomy 32:39; Psalm 107:20). David is extolling God for bringing him back from a near-death experience.

5. HIS ANGER IS BUT FOR A MOMENT: This stark contrast constitutes one of the most worshipful testimonies from the Scriptures (see the principle in Isaiah 54:7–8; John 16:20–22; 2 Corinthians 4:17).

6. "I SHALL NEVER BE MOVED": David recalls his previous independent attitude and arrogant talk. God had warned the nation and its leaders about such sinfully myopic outlooks (see Deuteronomy 8:11–20; note sample failures in Deuteronomy 32:15; 2 Chronicles 32:25; Jeremiah 22:21; Hosea 13:6; Daniel 4:28–37). By the grace of God, David woke up to the fact that he was acting like his arrogant adversaries (see Psalm 10:6).

8–10. I CRIED OUT TO YOU: A familiar argument for preservation of life (see Psalms 6:5; 28:1; 88:10–12; 115:17; Isaiah 38:18–19).

12. MY GLORY: Now with renewed perspective (contrast verse 6), David recognizes that all he is and has is due to God's unmerited grace (see verse 7a).

THE LORD A FORTRESS IN ADVERSITY: Psalm 31 contains more of David's problems, prayers, and praises. David will again walk a road that takes him from anguish to assurance.

31:1. IN YOU, O LORD, I PUT MY TRUST: Within the two settings of Psalm 31, the psalmist's testimonies passionately celebrate the sufficiencies of God: (1) the original, private setting (verses 1–18); and (2) the ultimate, public setting (verses 19–24).

2. BOW DOWN YOUR EAR TO ME. This is a bold "pay-attention-to-my-prayer" demand (see Psalm 102:2).

3. FOR YOUR NAME'S SAKE: The language resembles that of Psalm 23:1–3, except it now comes packaged with prayer requests.

5. INTO YOUR HAND: This is applied to both the lesser David and the greater David (see Luke 23:46). Here, it involves the common denominator of trust. This is a metaphor depicting God's power and control (see verse 15a; contrast verses 8, 15b).

6. I HAVE HATED: See Psalm 26:5 on the proper basis for such hatred (also Psalm 139:21).

USELESS IDOLS: This is a common designation for false gods (see Deuteronomy 32:21; 1 Kings 16:13; Jeremiah 10:15; 14:22; 16:19; 18:15; Jonah 2:8). On the foolishness of idolatry, see Habakkuk 2:18–20.

9–10. MY EYE WASTES AWAY . . . MY BONES WASTE AWAY: These terms quite frequently are employed metaphorically to convey the nonphysical impact of trials and tribulations.

11. I AM A REPROACH: The psalmist was a reproach to adversaries and personal acquaintances alike, a very painful alienation (see Psalm 88:8, 18).

13. FEAR IS ON EVERY SIDE: See Jeremiah 6:25; 20:3, 10; 46:5; 49:29; Lamentations 2:22.

THEY SCHEME: On such wicked plotting, see Jeremiah 11:19; 18:23.

16. MAKE YOUR FACE SHINE UPON YOUR SERVANT: This is a request for a personal application of the blessing of Numbers 6:25 (see also Psalms 4:6; 67:1; 80:3, 7, 19; 119:135).

17. LET THE WICKED BE ASHAMED: On their shame but not his, see Psalm 25:2, 3, 20; Jeremiah 17:18.

18–20. LET THE LYING LIPS BE PUT TO SILENCE: His enemies exhibit signs of "mouth" disease.

19. YOUR GOODNESS: As in the case of His other attributes, God being perfectly good is the ground for His doing good things (see Psalm 119:68).

23. LOVE THE LORD: Biblical love includes an attitudinal response and demonstrated obedience (see Deuteronomy 6:4, 5; 10:12; John 14:15, 21; 15:10; 2 John 6). The assurance of both reward and retribution is a biblical maxim (e.g., Deuteronomy 7:9–10).

24. BE OF GOOD COURAGE: A singular form of this plural imperative was addressed to Joshua in 1:7. It is used nearly twenty times in the Old Testament, particularly in anticipation of battle.

THE JOY OF FORGIVENESS: *Psalm 32 was classified by the early church as one of seven penitential psalms (the others are Psalms 6; 38; 51; 102; 130; 143). Among these, this psalm and Psalm 51 stand out as confessional giants.*

[A CONTEMPLATION]: This heading introduces a new technical term. It could indicate that Psalm 32 was a "contemplative poem," or a "psalm of understanding," or a "skillful psalm."

32:1. BLESSED IS HE: Historically related to the life of David, especially in connection with the Bathsheba episode (se 2 Samuel 11–12), this psalm would have been preceded by Psalm 51. Life's most important lessons about sin, confession, and forgiveness are skillfully shared by David in this psalm through two avenues of approach: (1) remembering these lessons, including lessons about results (verses 1–2), lessons about resistance (verses 3–4), lessons about responses (verse 5); and (2) relaying these lessons, including about responses (verses 6–7), lessons about resistance (verses 8–9), and lessons about results (verses 10–11).

1–2. TRANSGRESSION . . . SIN . . . INIQUITY: Three key Old Testament words for sin occur, appearing respectively as rebellion, failure, and perversion.

3–4. WHEN I KEPT SILENT, MY BONES GREW OLD: These are vivid descriptions of the physical effects of David's impenitent state.

5. I ACKNOWLEDGED MY SIN: David picks up the key terms that he had used to describe sin in verses 1–2; but now, in a context of personal confession, he identifies those heinous affronts to the person of God as his own. On the priority of confession, see Proverbs 28:13; 1 John 1:8–10.

6. EVERYONE WHO IS GODLY SHALL PRAY TO YOU: David slips right back into his teaching mode in this verse, emphasizing that every person who knows the grace of God should not presume upon that grace by putting off confession.

8. INSTRUCT . . . TEACH . . . GUIDE: This terminology applies to biblical wisdom.

9. HORSE . . . MULE: In other words, "Don't be stubborn." Such animals are used as pointed illustrations of this sin (see Proverbs 26:3; Isaiah 1:3; James 3:3).

Read Psalms 38–39, noting the key words and phrases indicated below.

PRAYER IN TIME OF CHASTENING: In many ways, David's laments in Psalm 38 parallel those of Job. David's perspective is that his painful plight is due, at least in part, to his personal sin. His prayers surround a core of intense lament.

[TO BRING TO REMEMBRANCE]: Literally, "to cause to remember" (see the title to Psalm 70). The psalmist either (1) reminds God of his plight so that He might act, or (2) reminds himself and the community of his historic predicament so that both he and they would fervently pray in similar contexts of acute suffering.

38:1. DO NOT REBUKE ME: See Psalms 6:1; 39:11; Jeremiah 31:18. Organizationally, David's opening and closing prayers in Psalm 38 relate to the onslaughts by his enemies: (1) introductory prayer (verses 1–2); (2) first onslaught, the enemy within (verses 3–10); (3) second onslaught, enemies without (verses 11–20); (4) concluding prayers (verses 21–22).

2. YOUR ARROWS PIERCE ME: The language relates to the divine Warrior motif. On God as Archer, see Deuteronomy 32:23; Job 6:4; 16:13; Psalm 7:12; Lamentations 3:12–13.

5. MY FOOLISHNESS: On culpable ethical folly, see Psalm 69:5. David views this as the reason for the divine chastisements of verses 3ff.

11. LOVED ONES . . . FRIENDS . . . RELATIVES: Those near and dear to the psalmist had abandoned him to his adversity, adding insult to injury.

13–14. IN WHOSE MOUTH IS NO RESPONSE: The ultimate example of nonresponse to tauntings and torturings may be seen in the Suffering Servant of Isaiah 53:7; see also 1 Peter 2:23.

19–20. I FOLLOW WHAT IS GOOD: Although he had confessed personal sins, the psalmist remained legally innocent in comparison with his persecutors.

> PRAYER FOR WISDOM AND FORGIVENESS: Psalm 39 is an exceptionally heavy lament. It also carries on the "here-today, gone-tomorrow" emphasis of Psalm 37 with a new twist—an application to all people, especially the psalmist.

[To JEDUTHUN]: This is most likely a specifically designated worship director (see 1 Chronicles 9:16; 16:37ff; 25:1–3; Nehemiah 11:17).

39:1. I WILL GUARD MY WAYS . . . I WILL RESTRAIN MY MOUTH. The form of these expressions in this verse intimate strong volitional commitments. In this lament, David will break his initial silence with two rounds of requests and reflections about the brevity and burdens of life. The organization of the psalm is as follows: (1) introduction—David's silence (verses:1–3); (2) round one—the brevity and burdens of life, including David's request for perspective (verse 4), David's reflection on perspective (verses 5–6); (3) round two—the brevity and burdens of life, including David's reflection on hope (verse 7), his request and reflection on providence (verses 8–11), and his request for relief (verses 12–13).

LEST I SIN WITH MY TONGUE: This sinning could have been in one or both of two ways: (1) directly, by criticizing God for not bringing retribution on the wicked, and/or (2) indirectly, by complaining in the hearing of the wicked.

2. MY SORROW WAS STIRRED UP: David's silence did not ease his pain; it seemed to make it all the worse.

3. MY HEART WAS HOT WITHIN ME: See Jeremiah's predicament in Jeremiah 20:9.

THEN I SPOKE WITH MY TONGUE: Contrast the silence of verse 1. Yet David did not violate the conditions of his original commitment, since he did not vent before people, but unloaded his burdens before God (see verses 4ff.).

4. THE MEASURE OF MY DAYS: For similar prayers about the brevity and burdens of life, see Job 6:11; 7:7; 14:13; 16:21–22; Psalm 90:12; Ecclesiastes 2:3.

5. HANDBREADTHS: The psalmist measures the length of his life with the smallest popular measuring unit of ancient times (see 1 Kings 7:26). See also "four fingers" (i.e., about 2.9 inches) in Jeremiah 52:21.

AND MY AGE IS AS NOTHING BEFORE YOU: On "measuring" God's age, see Psalm 90:2.

VAPOR: For the same Hebrew word, see Ecclesiastes 1:2ff, translated as "vanity" (a total of thirty-eight occurrences of this term are in Ecclesiastes); and Psalm 144:4, translated as "breath." On this concept in the New Testament, see James 4:14.

6. SURELY THEY BUSY THEMSELVES IN VAIN: On the futility and irony of this phenomenon, see Job 27:16 in context; see also Ecclesiastes 2:18–23; Luke 12:16–20.

9. I WAS MUTE: In this verse, the terminology of Psalms 38:13 and 39:2 reappears, accompanied by the theology of Job 42.

11. LIKE A MOTH: The moth normally represented one of the most destructive creatures; but here, the delicacy of the moth is intended (see Job 13:28; Isaiah 50:9; 51:8; Matthew 6:19ff.).

12. STRANGER . . . SOJOURNER: He considers himself to be a temporary guest and squatter in the presence of God. On the terminology, see Leviticus 25:23; Deuteronomy 24:19ff; 1 Chronicles 29:15; Psalm 119:19. For the concept in the New Testament, see Hebrews 11:13; 1 Peter 2:11.

13. REMOVE YOUR GAZE FROM ME: This stark request is parallel in its intention with verse 10.

Read Psalm 51, noting the key words and phrases indicated below.

A PRAYER OF REPENTANCE: Psalm 51, along with Psalm 32, were written by David after his affair with Bathsheba and his murder of her husband. It is the classic passage in the Old Testament on man's repentance and God's forgiveness of sin.

51:1. HAVE MERCY UPON ME, O GOD: The structure of this psalm is as follows: (1) David's plea for forgiveness (verses 1–2); (2) proffer of confession (verses 3–6); (3) prayer for moral cleanness (verses 7–12); (4) promise of renewed service (verses 13–17); and (5) petition for national restoration (verses 18–19).

LOVINGKINDNESS: To David's credit, he recognized how horrendous his sin against God was, blamed no one but himself, and begged for divine forgiveness. Yet even though he had sinned horribly, David knew that forgiveness was available, based on God's covenant love.

4. AGAINST YOU, YOU ONLY: David realized what every believer seeking forgiveness must know, that even though he had wronged Bathsheba and Uriah, his ultimate crime was against God and His holy law (see 2 Samuel 11:27). Paul quotes this verse in Romans 3:4.

5. BROUGHT FORTH IN INIQUITY: David also acknowledged his sin was not God's fault in any way (see verses 4b, 6), nor was it some aberration. Rather, the source of David's sin was a fallen, sinful disposition, i.e., his since conception.

7. HYSSOP: Old Testament priests used hyssop, a leafy plant, to sprinkle blood or water on a person being ceremonially cleansed from defilements such as leprosy or touching a dead body (see Leviticus 14:6ff; Numbers 19:16–19). Here, hyssop is a figure for David's longing to be cleansed from his moral defilement. In forgiveness, God washes away sin (see Psalm 103:12; Isaiah 1:16; Micah 7:19).

8. BONES: A figure of speech for the framework of the entire person. David was experiencing personal collapse under guilt (see Psalm 32:3–4).

11. YOUR HOLY SPIRIT FROM ME: This is a reference to the special Holy Spirit anointing on theocratic mediators.

12. GENEROUS SPIRIT: The Holy Spirit is generous, willing, and eager to uphold the believer.

16. YOU DO NOT DESIRE: Ritual without genuine repentance is useless. However, with a right heart attitude, sacrifices were acceptable (see verse 19).

UNLEASHING THE TEXT

1) What does Psalm 30 reveal about God's character, especially in connection with the confession and repentance of His people?

2) What are some similarities and differences between Psalm 51 (written first) and Psalm 32 (written second)? Specifically, what is the connection between David's confession in Psalm 51 and the subsequent result in Psalm 32?

3) Looking specifically at Psalm 51, how does it help readers understand the nature and process of repentance?

4) What can we learn about God's character in light of David's tone and language in Psalms 38 and 39?

EXPLORING THE MEANING

Repentance is an intentional act. Repentance is a familiar theme within the church, yet many Christians misunderstand what it is and what it requires. Specifically, many believe that repenting of sin is primarily "feeling sorry" for that sin—"feeling bad about it" and wanting to do better. This is not the case. Repentance is an intentional act that generally begins with an acknowledgment of the sinfulness of your sin, followed by a verbal confession of that sin and a renunciation of that sinful action. "I acknowledged my sin to You, and my iniquity I have not hidden. I said, 'I will confess my transgressions to the LORD,' and You forgave the iniquity of my sin" (32:5). "For I will declare my iniquity; I will be in anguish over my sin" (38:18). "Hear my prayer, O LORD, and give ear to my cry" (39:12). To repent means to acknowledge, confess, and renounce your sin before God. In addition, and what is often overlooked, is the fact that repentance involves a turning away from sin—an intentional choice to end your rebellion against God and obey His commandments.

True repentance leads to forgiveness. Why should Christians repent of their sin? First, because sin disrupts our communion with God and is harmful in our lives. Second, because God actively desires to forgive His children and sanctify them. True and genuine repentance is the door we walk through in order to receive that forgiveness, and by God's grace, He convicts us to repent of our sin. Psalm 51 is David's public confession after his sinful choices with Bathsheba and Uriah. Notably, he began that repentance by acknowledging God's forgiving character: "Have mercy upon me, O God, according to Your lovingkindness; according to the multitude of Your tender mercies, blot out my transgressions" (verse 1). In Psalm 32, David offered a timeline of sorts regarding his confession, repentance, and forgiveness. His initial attempts to hide his sin caused a rift in his relationship with God and a growing burden within his heart. Then, David made the choice to repent (see verse 5), and that repentance led to God's forgiveness: "I said, 'I will confess my transgressions to the LORD,' and You forgave the iniquity of my sin" (verse 5).

Repentance requires humility. In Psalm 38, David felt crushed by the weight of calamity—a situation he believed to be at least in part due to his personal sin. "I am troubled, I am bowed down greatly," he wrote. "I go mourning all the day long" (verse 6). His response was to cry out to God in humility and grief: "Do not forsake me, O LORD; O my God, be not far from me! Make haste to help me, O LORD, my salvation!" (verses 21–22). Similarly, Psalm 39 expresses David's awareness of his own smallness in comparison with God. David concluded that psalm with a poignant plea: "Remove Your gaze from me, that I may regain strength, before I go away and am no more" (verse 13). Repentance is a key element in our spiritual lives that constantly realigns our mind, affections, and will with God's. This requires humility because you must first recognize that you have violated His law, confess that sin, and renounce it by turning to Him. Beyond that, repentance requires humility because it is a gift from God, and in order to recognize that and praise Him for it, you must humble yourself.

REFLECTING ON THE TEXT

5) When was the last time you truly repented of your sin? Did it include an acknowledgment of the sinfulness of your sin? Did you confess it and renounce that sin? How has your life changed since that repentance?

_____

_____

_____

_____

_____

6) What prevents Christians from regularly practicing repentance?

_____

_____

_____

_____

7) David describes his sin as crushing and pressing him down. What does this tell us are some key indications that a person needs to repent?

_____

_____

_____

_____

_____

8) What are some specific ways to exhibit humility before God? Why does repentance require humility?

_____

_____

_____

_____

_____

_____

PERSONAL RESPONSE

9) Examine your own heart and discern what sins you need to acknowledge, confess, and renounce today.

_____

_____

_____

_____

_____

_____

10) What sins do you protect? Reflect on why you protect those sins, in light of who God is and what Christ has accomplished.

_____

_____

_____

_____

_____

_____

4

PSALMS DECLARING GOD'S STRENGTH

Psalms 42–44; 46–47

DRAWING NEAR

What are some of the different ways people rely upon their own strength? In comparison, what does Scripture teach about God's strength in the Christian life?

_____

_____

_____

_____

_____

_____

_____

THE CONTEXT

So far in this study, David wrote the majority of the psalms we have explored. In this section, however, we will meet a new group of contributors to the Psalms: the sons of Korah. It is quite probable that the sons of Korah were not the authors of these psalms, but rather their performers. For example, the title for Psalm 42 notes that it is "A Contemplation of the sons of Korah." This likely means that the sons of Korah were a part of the Levitical tribe who sang or otherwise performed these songs for the people.

Who were the sons of Korah? We do not know a lot about them definitively, but they carry an ignoble name. In the book of Numbers, we read that Korah was one of the leaders of a rebellion against God and Moses after the exodus. He challenged the authority of Moses and Aaron and the priesthood they had established. As a result, Korah and his followers were swallowed up by the ground during an earthquake (see Numbers 16:28–35).

The sons of Korah from the Psalms arose later, operating during the time of King David. They were likely legitimate descendants of that original Korah, who was a Levite. However, instead of leading rebellions, the sons of Korah participated in the work of the tabernacle and temple—work that included vocal worshiping and praising the Lord God through song. There are eleven total psalms attributed to the sons of Korah. We will study four of them in this section, in addition to Psalm 43, which was likely written by the same author as Psalm 42.

KEYS TO THE TEXT

Read Psalms 42–44, noting the key words and phrases indicated below.

> *YEARNING FOR GOD IN THE MIDST OF DISTRESSES: The occasion and situation behind the writing of Psalm 42 are historically unspecified. However, the psalmist's situation was obviously intense and greatly aggravated by his surrounding mockers.*

[A CONTEMPLATION]: As in the case of Psalms 9 and 10, Psalms 42 and 43 were originally probably one. Some ancient manuscripts put them together; Psalm 43 has no title, while the rest around it do. In form, Psalm 42 may be considered an individual lament. This psalm also exemplifies a primary characteristic of Book II of the Psalms, i.e., the preference of the ascription "God" (or parallels to it) for the deity. Consequently, Psalm 42 is a dirge of two stanzas: (1) stanza one, the psalmist sings of his drought (verses 1–5); and (2) stanza two, the psalmist sings of his drowning (verses 6–11).

42:1. AS THE DEER PANTS . . . SO PANTS: On this simile from nature, see Joel 1:20. In the psalmist's estimation, he is facing a severe, divine drought.

2. MY SOUL THIRSTS FOR GOD: On this desire for the water of God, see Psalm 36:8–9; Isaiah 41:17; 55:1; Jeremiah 2:13; 14:1–9; 17:13; John 4:10; 7:37–38; Revelation 7:17; 21:6; 22:1, 17.

4. WHEN I REMEMBER THESE THINGS, I POUR OUT MY SOUL: Such language also characterizes Jeremiah's Lamentations, indicating a heavy dirge.

On "pouring out one's soul" or "heart," see 1 Samuel 1:15; Psalm 62:8; Lamentations 2:19. These are attempts at trying to unburden oneself from intolerable pain, grief, and agony.

5. WHY ARE YOU CAST DOWN . . . AND . . . DISQUIETED: In this active introspection, the psalmist rebukes himself for his despondency.

6. THE LAND OF THE JORDAN . . . THE HEIGHTS OF HERMON . . . THE HILL MIZAR: The Mount Hermon and the Jordan notations refer to a location in northern Palestine, an area of headwaters which flow southward. These locations signal that a sharp contrast, in the word pictures describing the psalmist's change in condition, is imminent. He is about to move from drought to drowning (see verses 7ff.). The location and significance of Mount Mizar is not known.

7. DEEP . . . YOUR WATERFALLS . . . YOUR WAVES AND BILLOWS: The psalmist alleges that God is ultimately responsible for the oceans of trial in which he seems to be drowning.

8. THE LORD WILL COMMAND HIS LOVINGKINDNESS: This statement of confidence interrupts his laments (see their continuance in verses 9–10), providing a few gracious gulps of divine "air" under the cascading inundations of his trials and tormentors.

> PRAYER TO GOD IN TIME OF TROUBLE: *Psalm 43 might be*
> *understood as an epilogue to Psalm 42, as the psalmist moves*
> *away from introspection toward invocation.*

43:1 VINDICATE ME . . . PLEAD MY CAUSE: Literally, "Judge me, O God, and argue my case." This combination of legal terms demonstrates respectively that the psalmist was requesting God to be both his divine Judge (see Judges 11:27; 1 Samuel 24:12; Psalms 7:8; 26:1) and defense attorney (see Psalm 119:154; Proverbs 22:23; 23:11; Jeremiah 50:34; Lamentations 3:58). On both concepts together, as here, see 1 Samuel 24:15; Psalm 35:1, 24; Micah 7:9.

DELIVER ME: While the psalmist has moved away from introspection in Psalm 42 toward invocation in this psalm, it is clear that his problems had not ended, at least not fully and finally. Nevertheless, spiritual progress is evident. By interrelating the psalmist's two modes of communication in Psalm 43 and then by comparing them with the laments of Psalm 42, one observes indications of that progress as he continued to deal with his despondency. The structure of this psalm is as follows: (1) prayers to God, including righting wrongs (verses 1–2), and restoring "rights" (verses 3–4); and (2) the psalmist's "pep talks" to himself, including exhortation (verses 5a–b), and encouragement (verses 5c–d).

2. WHY ... WHY: Since God was his refuge of strength, the psalmist questioned why this apparent divine rejection and why his dejection.

3. YOUR LIGHT AND YOUR TRUTH! LET THEM LEAD ME; LET THEM BRING ME: These are bold personifications for divine guidance. The psalmist desired that these "messenger-attributes" divinely direct (see such "leading" and "guiding" in Genesis 24:48; Psalms 78:14, 53, 72; 107:30; Isaiah 57:18) so as to bring him successfully to his destination, i.e., Israel's designated place for worship.

5. WHY ... WHY ... HOPE: see Psalm 42:5, 11.

REDEMPTION REMEMBERED IN PRESENT DISHONOR: *Psalm 44*
is a national lament following some great, but historically
unidentifiable, defeat in battle.

[TO THE CHIEF MUSICIAN. A CONTEMPLATION OF THE SONS OF KORAH]: The words of this title are the same as those in the title of Psalm 42; however, in the Hebrew text their order is slightly different (literally, "To the Chief Musician, of the Sons of Korah, a Contemplation").

44:1. WE ... OUR ... US: Throughout this psalm, there are subtle shifts between speakers of the first person plural (i.e., "we" and "us"; see verses 1–3, 5, 7, 8, 9–14, 17–22) and the first person singular (i.e., "I" or "my"; see verses 4, 6, 15, 16). This may indicate that the psalm was originally sung antiphonally with alterations coming from both the beaten king-general and his defeated nation. The prayers of verses 23–26 may have been offered in unison as a climax. By employing three time frames in Psalm 44, the psalmist tries to understand and deal with a national tragedy: (1) focus on the past—the shock of this nation's tragedy (see verses 1–8); (2) focus on the present—the inscrutability of this national tragedy (see verses 9–22); and (3) focus on the future—a prayer for an end to this national tragedy (see verses 23–26).

WE HAVE HEARD: There was a rich tradition about God's great acts that the nation's fathers had passed on. Indeed, the rehearsal of holy history was commanded (see Exodus 10:1–2; 12:26ff; 13:14ff; Deuteronomy 6:20ff; Joshua 4:6ff; Psalm 78:3).

2. YOU PLANTED: On the imagery of God's planting His people, see 2 Samuel 7:10; Isaiah 5:1ff; Jeremiah 12:2; also see their being planted and taking root in Psalm 80:8–11.

3. FOR THEY DID NOT . . . BUT IT WAS YOUR RIGHT HAND: This is a brief historical summary of the theology of divine grace, intervention, and enablement (see Joshua 24:17–18).

4. COMMAND VICTORIES FOR JACOB: If the division of the Hebrew consonants is taken at a different point (as it is in some early versions), this line would better fit into the immediate context, reading: "You are my King, my God, who commands (or, orders) victories for Jacob." "Jacob," the original name of the ancient patriarch, is often used to designate the nation of Israel, especially in poetry.

5–8. THROUGH YOU . . . FOR I WILL NOT TRUST IN MY BOW . . . BUT YOU HAVE SAVED US: The defeated king-general picks up the theology of verse 3 and adds his personal commitment to it.

9. BUT YOU . . . DO NOT GO OUT WITH OUR ARMIES: The Lord God is viewed here as having apparently resigned His commission as the nation's divine Warrior.

11–16. YOU HAVE GIVEN . . . YOU SELL: These are graphic descriptions of God superintending the defeat and utter humiliation of the nation.

17–21. BUT WE HAVE NOT FORGOTTEN YOU . . . IF WE HAD FORGOTTEN THE NAME OF OUR GOD: The nation's recent defeat was painfully perplexing in view of their basic loyalty to God.

22. YET FOR YOUR SAKE: They had no specific answers, only this inescapable conclusion—by God's sovereign will, they were allowed to be destroyed by their enemies. See Paul's quote of this verse in Romans 8:36 and its general principle in Matthew 5:10–12; 1 Peter 3:13–17; 4:12–16.

23. AWAKE! . . . ARISE: See Psalm 35:23. God does not actually sleep. This is only in appearance to man's perception.

26 ARISE: See Numbers 10:35; Psalms 3:7; 7:6.

AND REDEEM US FOR YOUR MERCIES' SAKE: The psalm therefore comes full circle from the history of God's gracious redemption (verses 1–3) to the hope for the same in the near future (verse 26).

Read Psalms 46–47, noting the key words and phrases indicated below.

GOD THE REFUGE OF HIS PEOPLE AND CONQUEROR OF THE NATIONS: Psalm 46 extols the adequacy of God in facing threats from nature and the nations. The psalmist declares that God indeed protects His people upon the earth.

[A SONG FOR ALAMOTH]: The new element in this title is "Alamoth." The early Greek translation (the Septuagint) interprets this technical term as "hidden things." However, the Hebrew word normally has to do with "girls" or "young maidens." Consequently, the most likely conjecture about this phrase is that it is a technical musical notation, possibly indicating a song which was to be sung with female voices at a higher range.

46:1. GOD IS OUR REFUGE AND STRENGTH: Psalm 46 was the scriptural catalyst for Martin Luther's great hymn "A Mighty Fortress Is Our God." This psalm also launches a trilogy of psalms (i.e., 46; 47; 48); they are all songs of triumph. Furthermore, it has also been grouped among the so-called "songs of Zion" (Psalms 48; 76; 84; 87; 122). The major burden of Psalm 46 is that God provides stability for His people who live in two unstable environments: (1) that of nature (verses 1–3); and (2) that of the nations (verses 4–11).

2. EVEN THOUGH THE EARTH BE REMOVED: That is, "When earth changes and when mountains move (or) shake (or) totter (or) slip" (see the language of Isaiah 24:19–20; 54:10; Haggai 2:6). These are poetic allusions to earthquakes. Since "the earth" and "mountains" are regarded by men as symbols of stability, when they "dance" great terror normally ensues. But when the most stable becomes unstable, there should be "no fear" because of the transcendent stability of God.

3. THOUGH ITS WATERS ROAR: This is an illustration of powerfully surging and potentially destructive floods of waters. These will not erode God's protective fortifications.

4. THERE IS A RIVER WHOSE STREAMS: These words about refreshing waters contrast with those about the threatening torrents of verse 3. The garden of paradise concept is often mentioned in ancient Near Eastern literature, but most importantly, it appears in the biblical revelation, especially the "bookends" of Genesis 2:10 and Revelation 22:1–2.

THE CITY OF GOD: These words, in their present setting, refer to Jerusalem, God's chosen earthly residence (see Psalm 48:1–2; Isaiah 60:14).

5–6. SHE SHALL NOT BE MOVED: These verses pick up some of the key terms about moving, slipping, tottering, sliding, and roaring from verses 1–3. However, because of the presence of God, the forces of nature and the nations are no longer a threat to the people of God who dwell with Him.

7. THE LORD OF HOSTS IS WITH US: The precious, personal presence (see "God with us" in Isaiah 7:14; 8:8, 10) of the divine Warrior (see "LORD of hosts" or "armies," e.g., Psalms 24:10; 48:8; 59:5) secures the safety of His people.

8. DESOLATIONS: This word not only characterizes God's past exploits but is also employed in various "Day of the Lord" contexts (e.g., Isaiah 13:9; Hosea 5:9; Zephaniah 2:15).

10. BE STILL, AND KNOW THAT I AM GOD: These twin commands to not panic and to recognize His sovereignty are probably directed to both His nation for comfort and all other nations for warning.

> PRAISE TO GOD, THE RULER OF THE EARTH: *The main concepts of Psalm 47 develop around key words and phrases (e.g., "peoples" and "nations"; "earth" and "all the earth"; and "king" or "reigning [as king]"). The major message of Psalm 47 is that God is the unique Sovereign over all.*

47:1. OH, CLAP YOUR HANDS: Structurally, there are two choruses of worship in Psalm 47 which celebrate the universal kingship of the Lord God Most High: (1) first chorus—God as the victorious King-Warrior, including a call to worship (verse 1), and causes for worship (verses 2–5); and (2) second chorus—God as the sovereign King-Governor, including a call to worship (verse 6), causes for worship (verses 7–9b), and a code of worship (verse 9c).

ALL YOU PEOPLES: The call to worship is universal.

3. HE WILL SUBDUE: Or, "He subdues," i.e., an axiomatic truth about the past, present, and future.

4. HE WILL CHOOSE: Again, "He chooses" serves as a timeless truth. See the election of Israel in Deuteronomy 7:6ff; Psalm 135:4. On the land of promise as "inheritance," see Deuteronomy 32:8–9; Psalm 105:11. Individual election is explicitly taught in Ephesians 1:4 and 1 Peter 1:2, amongst other texts.

THE EXCELLENCE OF JACOB WHOM HE LOVES: The excellence or pride of Jacob also refers to the land of Canaan (see the term illustratively in Isaiah 13:19; Isaiah 60:15; Nahum 2:2). "Whom He loves" is signal terminology for God's special, elective, covenantal love (see, e.g., Malachi 1:2ff). This special focus on God's covenant with Israel does not negate the bigger picture involving blessing to all nations sketched out in the original Abrahamic covenant of Genesis 12:1–3.

5. GOD HAS GONE UP WITH A SHOUT: The imagery likely refers to God's presence, after having gone into battle with His people, now ascending victoriously to His immanent "residence" on Mount Zion and to His transcendent residence in heaven. This procession with the ark of God was accompanied by great shouts and blasts of celebration in verses 5 and 6.

9. THE SHIELDS OF THE EARTH: This imagery stands parallel with "the princes of the people." Illustratively, there may be a loose analogy to God's sovereignly appointed, human governors (see Romans 13:1–7) as protectors for the masses.

UNLEASHING THE TEXT

1) Psalms 42 and 43 are often considered to be two halves of a single song. What are the connections between them?

_____

_____

_____

_____

2) Why was the author of Psalm 44 interested in God's strength?

_____

_____

_____

3) Cite some specific ways that Psalm 46 proclaims and instructs us about God's strength.

_____

_____

_____

_____

4) What evidence points to Psalm 47 being written for a corporate setting?

_____

_____

_____

_____

_____

EXPLORING THE MEANING

Worship must be a priority for followers of God. The sons of Korah were likely vocal performers rather than the official authors of the eleven psalms that bear their name. But even the existence of a group like them should give us pause. In the midst of a vast and complex sacrificial system—with different groups of the Levitical tribe tasked with all manner of jobs—one group was given the specific assignment of singing God's praises and leading others to do the same. Why? Because worship is a priority! When we rightly understand who God is and who we are, worship should naturally overflow through our lives—and through our lips. As we've seen, David made worship a priority. From the time he was an unknown shepherd all the way through his most glorious accomplishment as king, David worshiped God and helped others express their worship to God. Similarly, in our journey of following Christ, we must always remember that worshiping God is more than singing a few songs every Sunday. Worship is the posture of our lives as we praise and appreciate our sovereign Lord.

We have access to God's strength. God uses His strength to bless those who follow Him, as Psalm 46 makes clear: "God is our refuge and strength, a very present help in trouble" (verse 1). There are some critical words in that verse. First, God is "our" refuge and strength. He extends His strength to us. Second, God's strength is "very present." God is not like the capricious kings of old who would only intervene on the side of justice when forced to do so or when they saw personal benefit to it. Instead, God is present with us. What should the result of that strength be in our lives? The psalmist said it best in verse 2: "Therefore we will not fear."

God often uses His strength to forge peace. God is holy, He seeks justice, and His wrath is a legitimate expression of His justice. Those truths are frightening when connected with God's unparalleled power and unstoppable strength. However, it's also true that God often uses His power to establish peace and end the consequences of violence and strife, which is what the author of Psalm 46 emphasized. Throughout the song, he described God's powerful interventions in the world. Yet the psalmist was careful to illustrate the end result of God expending His strength: "He makes wars cease to the end of the earth; He breaks the bow and cuts the spear in two; He burns the chariot in the fire" (verse 9). On that last point, chariots were the supreme weapons of war in the ancient world. So, burning or melting chariots was akin to removing the most brutal weapons of an enemy's arsenal. God is strong, yet that should cause us to trust rather than fear Him because God often uses His strength to end wars, cease struggles, and build peace. Of course, the best example of Him doing so is Christ's death on the cross—a supreme act of strength that has accomplished redemption for those who repent and believe in Christ, which leads to peace with God.

REFLECTING ON THE TEXT

5)   How can you make worship a priority in your daily life?

_____

_____

_____

_____

_____

_____

_____

6)   God uses His strength to bless us. How has His strength blessed you, specifically? Do you continue to trust in His strength and not your own?

_____

_____

_____

_____

_____

_____

_____

_____

7) Think of specific things you know you were able to accomplish only because of God's strength working for you. How do those things cause you to praise God like the psalmist did?

_____

_____

_____

_____

_____

8) Why is strength a necessary element in lasting peace?

_____

_____

_____

_____

PERSONAL RESPONSE

9) Why is God's strength necessary in general? Why is God's strength necessary for your own life?

_____

_____

_____

_____

10) How can you better trust God's strength? What is required in order for Him to increase and for you to decrease?

_____

_____

_____

_____

_____

5

PSALMS OF TRUST IN GOD
Psalms 57–58; 61–63; 66

DRAWING NEAR
Why is trust important? What makes God trustworthy?

_____

_____

_____

_____

_____

_____

_____

_____

_____

THE CONTEXT
We saw in previous lessons that the book of Psalms is a collection of 150 individual songs and poems written by many different authors across a wide span of time. These songs and poems cover different themes, including the need to trust in God, which we will cover in this lesson. The book of Psalms is generally included in the literary genre of wisdom literature.

It is helpful to understand that the biblical book of Psalms is divided into five sub-books. Book I includes Psalms 1–41, most (or potentially all) of which were written by David. Book II includes Psalms 42–72 and contains most of the songs connected with the sons of Korah. Book III includes Psalms 73–89 and contains most of the songs composed by Asaph, one of David's choirmasters. Book IV includes Psalms 90–106 and contains the only psalm written by Moses. Book V includes Psalms 107–150 and contain the "Psalms of Ascent," which are believed to have been sung by Jewish pilgrims as they "ascended" to Jerusalem during the festivals.

In this lesson, we will conclude our study of Book II by exploring several psalms written by David. Some of these were written either during or as a response to notable historical events. For example, it is believed that David wrote Psalm 57 while hiding out in the wilderness from King Saul, who wanted to kill him (see 1 Samuel 23:13–29). Psalms 61 and 62 were likely written during the national revolt led by David's son, Absalom (see 2 Samuel 15:1–18:18).

Keys to the Text

Read Psalms 57–58, noting the key words and phrases indicated below.

> Prayer for Safety from Enemies: *Psalm 57 represents another lament expressing supreme confidence in the Lord in the midst of calamitous circumstances.*

["Do Not Destroy"]: These are possibly the opening words of a known song, implying that this psalm should be sung to the same tune.

57:1. my soul trusts in You: Even though David finds himself hiding from Saul (as the title to the psalm suggests), he knows that his real refuge is not in the walls of the cave (see 1 Samuel 22:1; 24:3) but in the shadow of God's wings. The structure of this psalm is as follows: (1) David's plea for protection (verses 1–6); and (2) David's proffering of praise (verses 7–11).

the shadow of Your wings: Metaphorically, God cares for His own as a mother bird protects its young. Symbolically, there may be a reference here to the cherubim wings on the ark of the covenant, where God was specifically present (see Exodus 37:1–16; Psalms 17:8; 36:7; 61:4; 63:7; 91:1, 4).

I will make my refuge: When life becomes bizarre, only a person's relationship with his God calms the soul.

2. God Most High: God is transcendent, elevated far above His creation and all powerful.

PERFORMS ALL THINGS FOR ME: God's transcendence (see verse 2a) never removes Him from intimate involvement in His people's lives.

4. MY SOUL IS AMONG LIONS: The wicked are pictured as menacing animals, ready to destroy their prey with their razor-edged teeth (see Psalms 7:2; 10:9; 17:12; 22:13).

SET ON FIRE: The wicked are like a consuming fire.

5. BE EXALTED, O GOD: A truly godly person wants God's glory to be exhibited more than he wants his own personal problems to be solved.

6. A NET ... A PIT: This pictures setting a trap, as a hunter might entangle an animal's feet with a net.

7–11. MY HEART IS STEADFAST: These verses were borrowed by David for Psalm 108:1–5.

8. MY GLORY: This refers to the mind, that rational, intellectual, emotional part of a person which interacts with and praises God.

I WILL AWAKEN THE DAWN: The psalmist cannot wait until morning to praise the Lord for all of His blessings. He must wake up the dawn (personified) so that he can praise the Lord.

9. THE PEOPLES ... NATIONS: These are references to Gentiles, nations which would not normally know Jehovah God.

10. UNTO THE HEAVENS: David is thinking as broadly (see verse 9) and as highly (see verses 10–11) as he can. God's mercy, truth, and glory are immense and unfathomable (see Romans 11:33; Ephesians 3:17–18).

> THE JUST JUDGMENT OF THE WICKED: *As a lament against tyranny, the first half of Psalm 58 rehearses a series of charges against wicked leaders and judges, while the second half is an imprecatory prayer that they be obliterated.*

58:1. DO YOU INDEED SPEAK RIGHTEOUSNESS: The structure of this psalm is as follows: (1) an indictment of unjust leaders (verses 1–5); and (2) an imprecation against unjust leaders (verses 6–11). In the end, the psalmist is certain that God will act with ultimate justice.

SILENT ONES: The leaders were silent when they should have spoken up for righteousness.

2. WEIGH OUT: These rulers meditate on the strategy for wicked schemes.

3. AS SOON AS THEY ARE BORN: All people are born totally depraved. Without being made new creatures in Christ by God's power, they are prevented by their wicked nature from pleasing God (see Psalm 51:5; Romans 3:9–18; 2 Corinthians 5:17).

4. THEIR POISON: The words and actions of these tyrants are like poisonous venom in a serpent's fangs.

DEAF COBRA: Like a cobra which cannot hear its charmer are these stubborn rulers, who ignore all encouragements to righteousness.

6. BREAK THEIR TEETH . . . FANGS: The psalmist prays that the means of doing evil would be destroyed.

7. FLOW AWAY AS WATERS: An imprecatory prayer that the tyrants would disappear like water seeping into sand in a dry wadi.

ARROWS . . . CUT IN PIECES: Apparently, this is a prayer that the intentions of evil would be rendered as ineffective as broken arrows.

8. SNAIL WHICH MELTS AWAY: A simile for that which is transitive, perhaps facetiously based on the idea that a snail depletes itself in its own trail as it moves along.

9. BEFORE YOUR POTS . . . THORNS: An obscure metaphor implying swiftness. The Lord will quickly destroy the wicked rulers.

10. WASH HIS FEET IN THE BLOOD: The point of the figure is that the wicked will eventually be defeated and the righteous will share with the Lord in His victory.

11. GOD WHO JUDGES IN THE EARTH: In the end, the righteous will see that Jehovah is not indifferent to injustices.

Read Psalms 61–63, noting the key words and phrases indicated below.

> *ASSURANCE OF GOD'S ETERNAL PROTECTION: Psalm 61 is rich in metaphors and references to God's covenants with Israel. David once again demonstrates a godly response to overwhelming and depressing developments in life.*

61:1. HEAR MY CRY: David may have written this wonderful psalm when his own son, Absalom, temporarily drove him away from his throne in Israel (see 2 Samuel 15–18). The structure of the psalm is as follows: (1) David's cry for help (verses 1–2); (2) his confidence in God (verses 3–7); and (3) his commitment to loyalty to God (verse 8).

2. FROM THE END OF THE EARTH: David's absence from his homeland compounds his feelings of discouragement and exhaustion. The phrase also hints at feelings of estrangement from God.

MY HEART IS OVERWHELMED: David's hope and courage were failing.

THE ROCK THAT IS HIGHER: David expresses his disregard of personal autonomy and his reliance on his God in this metaphor for refuge.

3. STRONG TOWER: One of four figures of speech in verses 3 and 4 for security; the strong towers stabilized the city walls and served as places of defense and refuge.

5. HERITAGE: This refers to the benefits, including life in the Promised Land (see Deuteronomy 28–30), of participating in a covenant with God.

6. PROLONG THE KING'S LIFE: In the immediate context, David prays for himself in his struggle with Absalom. Beyond this, it is a prayer for the continuity of the divinely established monarchy. Because he realized that one of his descendants would be the Messiah, David sometimes does not distinguish himself from the messianic dynasty.

7. FOREVER: The Davidic covenant guaranteed that, on the basis of God's merciful and faithful dealings with David and the nation, David's descendants would rule on the throne of Israel forever (see 2 Samuel 7; Psalms 40:11; 89:4, 33–37).

8. DAILY PERFORM MY VOWS: As a regular means of expressing thanksgiving for prayers answered, the psalmist promised daily obedience to his Lord (see Psalm 56:12).

A CALM RESOLVE TO WAIT FOR THE SALVATION OF GOD:
David wrote Psalm 62 while facing treason from someone.
Absalom's rebellion is again possibly the setting.

[TO JEDUTHUN]: An official temple musician. See note on Psalm 39.

62:1. MY SOUL SILENTLY WAITS FOR GOD: Silence indicates trust that is both patient and uncomplaining (see verse 5).

FROM HIM COMES MY SALVATION: David embraces the problem of his adversaries forthrightly (see verses 3–4), but his thoughts focus primarily on God (see Philippians 4:4–13). The structure of the psalm is as follows: (1) affirming

God's covenant relationship (verses 1–2, 5–6); (2) confronting one's treasonous adversaries (verses 3–4); (3) trusting God's sovereignty (verses 7–10); and (4) praising God's power and mercy (verses 11–12).

2. GREATLY MOVED: This means "shaken," or "demoralized."

3. LEANING WALL AND A TOTTERING FENCE: A metaphor for imminent collapse. Some apply it to the victim, but as translated here, it refers to the attacker.

6. I SHALL NOT BE MOVED: David demonstrates his increased confidence in the Lord. At first, he would not be "greatly moved" (verse 2). Here, on second thought, he would not be moved at all.

9. LOW DEGREE . . . HIGH DEGREE: All men, regardless of social status, are woefully inadequate objects of trust.

> JOY IN THE FELLOWSHIP OF GOD: *Psalm 63 expresses David's*
> *intense love for his Lord. The psalm was written while he was in*
> *the Judean wilderness, either during his flight from Saul or, more*
> *likely, from his son Absalom.*

63:1. YOU ARE MY GOD: David writes of his love for God from the perspective of these grammatical tenses: (1) present—seeking God's presence (verses 1–5); (2) past—remembering God's power (verses 6–8); and (3) future—anticipating God's judgment (verses 9–11).

1. EARLY WILL I SEEK YOU: Eagerness to be with the Lord in every situation is more in view than the time of day.

MY SOUL THIRSTS: David longs for God's presence like a wanderer in a desert longs for water.

IN A DRY AND THIRSTY LAND: David writes this psalm while hiding in the wilderness of Judea but longing to be back worshiping in Jerusalem.

3. BETTER THAN LIFE: God's covenant love is more valuable to David than life itself (cf. Philippians 1:21; Acts 20:24).

4. LIFT UP MY HANDS: As an Old Testament posture of prayer, the upheld hands pictured both the ascent of prayer and the readiness to receive every good gift which comes from God (see James 1:17). It was, thus, a posture of trust in God alone.

5. MARROW AND FATNESS: A metaphor comparing the spiritual and emotional satisfaction of the divine presence with the satisfaction of rich banquet food.

8. MY SOUL FOLLOWS CLOSE BEHIND YOU: In response to God's repeated invitation to "hold fast" to Him (see Deuteronomy 4:4; 10:20; 13:4), the psalmist clings to God. This signifies David's unfailing commitment to his Lord.

9. LOWER PARTS OF THE EARTH: A reference to the realm of the dead.

10. JACKALS: Scavengers, feasting on unburied bodies.

11. WHO SWEARS BY HIM: The Mosaic covenant instructed this practice expressing loyalty to the true God alone (see Deuteronomy 6:13; 10:20; 1 Kings 8:31; Jeremiah 12:16).

Read Psalm 66, noting the key words and phrases indicated below.

> *PRAISE TO GOD FOR HIS AWESOME WORKS: Psalm 66 begins with group praise and then focuses on individual worship. It rehearses some of the miracles in Israel's history and testifies that God has always been faithful in the midst of serious troubles.*

66:1. A JOYFUL SHOUT: A shout of loyalty and homage, as in 1 Samuel 10:24. The structure of this psalm is as follows: (1) communal hymn of praise to God—for future glory (verses 1–4), for previous faithfulness (verses 5–7), and for continual protection (verses 8–12); and (2) an individual hymn of praise to God—through fulfilled vows (verses 13–15), and for answered prayer (verses 16–20).

4. ALL THE EARTH SHALL WORSHIP YOU: This praise is not only an acknowledgment of God's universal lordship but also an intimation of the people's belief in a future, worldwide kingdom where God will be worshiped (see Isaiah 66:23; Zechariah 14:16; Philippians 2:10–11).

6. SEA ... RIVER: A reference to the crossing of the Red Sea and, possibly, the Jordan River. The Old Testament writers considered the Red Sea crossing the ultimate demonstration of God's power as well as His care for Israel.

9. FEET TO BE MOVED: God had prevented them from prematurely slipping into the realm of the dead.

10. REFINED US AS SILVER: God had brought the nation through purifying trials.

11. BROUGHT US INTO THE NET: The psalmist speaks of a hunter's net or snare as a metaphor for some extremely difficult situations into which God had brought Israel.

12. RIDE OVER OUR HEADS: A picture of a hostile army riding in victory over Israel's defeated troops.

13. PAY YOU MY VOWS: Paying the vows is spelled out in the following verses as offering sacrifices of dedication which had been previously promised God (see Leviticus 1; 22:18, 21; Psalms 56:12; 61:8; 65:1).

UNLEASHING THE TEXT

1) In Psalm 57, what reasons did David give for trusting God?

_____

_____

_____

_____

2) What are the key images in Psalm 62 and what do they communicate?

_____

_____

_____

_____

_____

3) As you read through these psalms, what obstacles did David encounter that could have hindered his ability to trust God?

_____

_____

_____

_____

_____

4) Psalm 66 is an explosion of praise. What is the connection it gives between trusting God and praising God?

_____

_____

_____

_____

EXPLORING THE MEANING

We should be honest about our difficulties. As you read David's psalms, it quickly becomes clear that he poured himself and his experiences into his songs and reflections, refusing to sugarcoat his sorrows and joys. In short, he was honest about his emotions and experiences—especially when he wrote as a way of communicating with God. "My soul is among lions," he wrote in Psalm 57, "I lie among the sons of men who are set on fire, whose teeth are spears and arrows, and their tongue a sharp sword" (verse 4). David was also honest about those who wronged him: "Break their teeth in their mouth, O God! Break out the fangs of the young lions, O LORD!" (Psalm 58:6). Often, we equate spirituality with stoicism, believing that expressing emotions, fears, or doubts is akin to a lack of faith. As a result, we remain silent about our struggles. But in doing so, we forfeit a precious gift and disobey what God has called us to do, namely, seeking His help, just as David did.

We should trust in God, our Rock. As you read through the different psalms included in this lesson, you likely noticed that David relied heavily on a specific type of imagery during his descriptions of God: "From the end of the earth I will cry to You, when my heart is overwhelmed; lead me to the rock that is higher than I" (Psalm 61:2). "For You have been a shelter for me, a strong tower from the enemy" (verse 3). "He only is my rock and my salvation; He is my defense; I shall not be greatly moved" (Psalm 62:2). "In God is my salvation and my glory; the rock of my strength, and my refuge, is in God" (verse 7). David often described God as his "rock" or "shelter" or "a strong tower." In doing so, he rightly understood a key aspect of God's character: God does not change, nor can He be moved. For these reasons, among many others, God is worthy of our trust. As David wrote: "Trust in Him at all times, you people; pour out your heart before Him; God is a refuge for us" (Psalm 62:8).

We should trust God based on His previous and present faithfulness. When we think about trusting God, it's easy to interpret that concept in terms of a blind trust. Meaning, those who follow God know they are supposed to trust Him simply because He is God and the Bible says to trust Him. Although Scripture calls us to trust God because of who He is, it also bases that command on God's proven faithfulness. Specifically, His faithfulness in the past and even in our current moment. God's previous trustworthiness was the foundation for David's trust. "Because You have been my help," he wrote, "therefore in the shadow of Your wings I will rejoice. My soul follows close behind You; Your right hand upholds me" (Psalm 63:7–8). Psalm 66 is a burst of praise and worship to God because of God's mighty works on behalf of His people. God certainly is worthy of our trust simply because of His power, character, and authority. Yet we don't need to trust blindly. We can look back at the journey of our lives and make note of all those moments when God stepped in and worked on our behalf. Those moments are the foundation for our trust in Him.

REFLECTING ON THE TEXT

5) What does it mean to be honest with God? Does your honesty lead you to call upon God for help?

_____

_____

_____

_____

_____

_____

6) Why can it be difficult to trust God? What sin or sins frequently hinder you from seeking His help, comfort, and direction?

_____

_____

_____

_____

_____

7) What attributes of God necessitate His faithfulness?

_____

_____

_____

_____

8) What are some ways that God's faithfulness in the past helped you trust Him in the present?

_____

_____

_____

_____

_____

_____

PERSONAL RESPONSE

9) What should be your response if God desires to use your trial for your own good and His glory?

_____

_____

_____

_____

_____

10) How can you express God's trustworthiness to others, even this week?

_____

_____

_____

_____

_____

6

PSALMS OF GOD'S GOODNESS
Psalms 73–76; 78; 82

DRAWING NEAR
How does our culture define goodness? How does the Bible define it?

_____

_____

_____

_____

_____

_____

_____

_____

_____

_____

THE CONTEXT
In the previous lessons, we have covered Book I and Book II of Psalms. In this lesson we will begin to explore Book III, which includes Psalms 73–89. As noted in the introduction to this study, there is no discernable reason why Psalms is divided into its five books, though Jewish tradition alleged these divisions echoed the five books of Moses. Many authors have psalms in several books, for example, so they are not arranged by writer. Nor are they arranged by topic.

In regard to authorship, each of the psalms in this section is connected to a man named Asaph. We know little about the identity of Asaph except that he was a Levite, as were the sons of Korah, and a contemporary of David. We also know from 1 Chronicles 6:39 that Asaph was the leader of a specific tabernacle choir. Additionally, in 2 Chronicles 29:30, we read that he (along with David) was a skilled poet and singer.

It is possible that Asaph was not the direct author of the psalms but was the one charged with performing them—or perhaps leading his choir to perform them. This possibility is made more likely because Asaph's psalms seem to span a wide timeline. For example, Psalm 74 may have been written to mourn the destruction of Jerusalem and the temple by the Babylonians—an event that took place several hundred years after David and Asaph died. Regardless, the goodness of God is a theme repeated in many of Asaph's psalms, and we will focus specifically on that theme in this lesson.

KEYS TO THE TEXT

Read Psalms 73–76, noting the key words and phrases indicated below.

THE TRAGEDY OF THE WICKED, AND THE BLESSEDNESS OF TRUST
IN GOD: In Psalm 73, the author contrasts the seeming prosperity
of the wicked with the difficulties of living a righteous life. Yet he
concludes it is the wicked, not the righteous, who have blundered.

73:2–3. MY FEET HAD ALMOST STUMBLED . . . I WAS ENVIOUS OF THE BOASTFUL: This psalm illustrates the results of allowing one's faith in God to be buried under self-pity. The psalmist became depressed when he saw the prosperity of the wicked. Beginning in verse 15, however, his attitude changes completely and he looks at life from the perspective of being under the control of a sovereign, holy God. The structure of this psalm is as follows: (1) perplexity over the prosperity of the wicked—their prosperity (verses 1–5), their pride (verses 6–9), and their presumption (verses 10–14); and (2) proclamation of the justice of God—His perspective (verses 15–17), His judgments (verses 18–20), and His guidance (verses 21–28).

4. NO PANGS IN THEIR DEATH: The wicked seem to go through life in good health, and then die a painless death.

9. TONGUE WALKS THROUGH THE EARTH: The insolent speech of the wicked can be heard anywhere one goes.

10. ARE DRAINED BY THEM: Those who associate with the wicked person "drink in" everything he declares (see Psalm 1).

11. IS THERE KNOWLEDGE IN THE MOST HIGH: The wicked insist on living as if God is not omniscient and does not know what happens on earth.

17. SANCTUARY OF GOD: As the psalmist worshiped God at the worship center, he began to understand God's perspective on the fate of the wicked. This is the turning point of the psalm.

20. DESPISE THEIR IMAGE: The wicked are like a bad dream which one forgets as soon as he awakens. Their well-being is fleeting.

22. LIKE A BEAST BEFORE YOU: The psalmist confesses his sin of evaluating life secularly and faithlessly.

27. PERISH . . . YOU HAVE DESTROYED: The psalmist concludes that those who abandon God and attempt to live an autonomous life based on self-chosen idols will eventually endure eternal death.

> *A PLEA FOR RELIEF FROM OPPRESSORS: Psalm 74 is a community lament expressing the agony of the people in the midst of the most excruciating of circumstances. It was bad enough that Israel's enemies had destroyed the temple (see 2 Kings 25); but even worse, it seemed to the psalmist that God had abandoned them.*

[OF ASAPH]: If this psalm reflects the destruction of the temple by Nebuchadnezzar in 586 BC, Asaph would have been dead by then. Thus, this title may mean that this psalm was written by or sung by a later Asaph choir.

74:1. WHY HAVE YOU CAST US OFF: The psalmist reminds God of His bond with Israel plus His past supernatural deeds to protect Israel and begs God to save His covenant nation now (see Psalm 137 and Lamentations 1–5). The structure of the psalm is as follows: (1) the terror of abandonment (verses 1–11); (2) the remembrance of omnipotence (verses 12–17); and (3) the plea for help (verses 18–23).

2. TRIBE OF YOUR INHERITANCE: The psalmist laments that even though God possessed Israel, He had not protected it.

3. LIFT UP YOUR FEET: An anthropomorphism meaning, "Hurry and come to examine the rubble."

4. THEIR BANNERS FOR SIGNS: The ravagers had set up their military and pagan religious banners in God's temple.

5. LIFT UP AXES: Like lumberjacks surrounded by trees, the enemy had destroyed everything in sight in the temple of God.

8. THE MEETING PLACES: God allowed only one sanctuary, and during Josiah's revival, the high places had been destroyed (see 2 Kings 22–23). This may be a reference to the several rooms of the temple or to non-sacrificial religious sites throughout the land.

9. OUR SIGNS: While hostile, pagan signs abounded (see verse 4), signs from God were nowhere to be seen (see Psalms 78:43; 86:17; 105:27) nor were prophets of God to be heard.

13. DIVIDED THE SEA: This is most likely a reference to God's creation activity, rather than to the parting of the Red Sea (see Genesis 1:6–8; Exodus 14:26–31).

SEA SERPENTS: This identifies whales, sharks, and other large sea creatures, including dinosaurs.

14. LEVIATHAN: This term appears in four other Old Testament texts (Job 3:8; 41:1; Psalm 104:26; Isaiah 27:1). In each case, Leviathan refers to a mighty creature that can overwhelm man but who is no match for God. Since this creature lives in the sea among ships (see Psalm 104:26), some form of sea monster, possibly an ancient dinosaur, is in view.

15. BROKE OPEN THE FOUNTAIN . . . FLOOD: This may refer to the universal flood (see Genesis 7:11), or it may describe creation (see Genesis 1:6–8).

17. SET ALL THE BORDERS: As Creator, God made day and night, also the seasons (see verse 16); He divided the land from the sea; and He even established national boundaries.

20. THE COVENANT: The people had apostatized (see Exodus 16:3–8). God, however, was still in an eternal covenant (the Abrahamic covenant) with the nation (see Genesis 17:1–8).

> THANKSGIVING FOR GOD'S RIGHTEOUS JUDGMENT: *In Psalm 75, the believing community asserts that in spite of physical, moral, and societal turmoil, God never loses control of the universe. He gives stability to life and will judge the wicked at the appropriate time.*

75:1. WE GIVE THANKS TO YOU: Structurally, the psalm revolves around three metaphors: (1) pillars of the earth (see verse 3); (2) horns (see verses 5, 6, 11); and (3) God's cup of wrath (verse 8). The psalm itself is broken into two themes:

(1) God's divine stability over the universe (verses 1–3); and (2) God's divine justice over the world (verses 4–10).

YOUR NAME IS NEAR: God's name represents His presence. The history of God's supernatural interventions on behalf of His people demonstrated that God was personally immanent. But Old Testament saints did not have the fullness of God's presence from permanent, personal indwelling of the Holy Spirit (see John 14:1, 16–17; 1 Corinthians 3:16; 6:19).

3. I SET UP ITS PILLARS FIRMLY: In uncertain times, God stabilizes societies through His common grace.

4. DO NOT LIFT UP THE HORN: The horn symbolized an animal's or human's strength and majesty (see Deuteronomy 33:17; Amos 6:13; Zechariah 1:18–21). Lifting up the horn apparently described a stubborn animal who kept itself from entering a yoke by holding its head up as high as possible. The phrase thus symbolized insolence or rebellion.

8. CUP: The cup of wrath describes God's judgment, which He forces down the throats of the wicked (see Job 21:20; Isaiah 51:17; Jeremiah 25:15–29; Matthew 20:22; 26:39).

10. HORNS . . . CUT OFF: To cut off the horns of the wicked would be to humble them (see verse 4).

THE MAJESTY OF GOD IN JUDGMENT: *Psalm 76 teaches that God will use His power for His people. It also includes eschatological overtones, when Jehovah will defeat His enemies and bring them into judgment.*

76:1. IN JUDAH GOD IS KNOWN: Some commentators, including the editors of the Septuagint, have suggested this psalm was written to celebrate the destruction of Sennacherib's Assyrian army in 701 BC, as well as the subsequent assassination of Sennacherib himself (see verses 5–6; see also 2 Kings 18–19; Isaiah 36–37). The structure of the psalm is as follows: (1) God's nearness to His people (verses 1–3); (2) God's deliverance of His people (verses 4–9); and (3) God's majesty to His people (verses 10–12).

3. BROKE THE ARROWS . . . SHIELD . . . SWORD: God destroyed the enemy's weapons.

4. MOUNTAINS OF PREY: Probably a poetic description of the attackers.

5. THE USE OF THEIR HANDS: God had crippled the enemy soldiers.

10. WRATH OF MAN SHALL PRAISE YOU: The railings against God and His people are turned into praise to God when God providentially brings the wicked down (see Isaiah 36:4–20; Acts 2:23; Romans 8:28).

12. CUT OFF THE SPIRIT OF PRINCES: God shatters the attitude of proud governmental leaders who rebel against Him.

Read Psalm 78, noting the key words and phrases indicated below.

> GOD'S KINDNESS TO REBELLIOUS ISRAEL: *The didactic Psalm 78 was written to teach the younger generation of the Israelite people just how gracious the Lord had been in the past in spite of their ancestors' rebellion and ingratitude.*

78:1. INCLINE YOUR EARS: The psalmist desired these children to learn well the theological interpretation of their nation's history so they would hopefully "not be like their fathers" (verse 8). The psalmist especially focuses on the history of the exodus. The structure of the psalm is as follows: (1) exhortation on the instruction of children (verses 1–11); (2) lecture on the graciousness of God (verses 12–72), which rehearses Israel's history (verses 12–39) and reiterates historical lessons (verses 40–72).

2. PARABLE: The word is used here in the broader sense of a story with moral and spiritual applications.

DARK SAYINGS: This is puzzling, ambiguous information. The lessons of history are not easily discerned correctly. For an infallible interpretation of history, there must be a prophet. The specific puzzle in Israel's history is the nation's rebellious spirit in spite of God's grace.

9. CHILDREN OF EPHRAIM: The act of treachery or apostasy by this largest of the northern tribes is not specifically identified in Israel's history.

12. FIELD OF ZOAN: The regions of Zoan, an Egyptian city.

13. WATERS STAND UP LIKE A HEAP: The parting of the Red Sea at the beginning of the exodus, which allowed Israel to escape from the Egyptian armies, was always considered by the Old Testament saints to be the most spectacular miracle of their history (see Exodus 14).

15. SPLIT THE ROCKS: Twice in the wilderness, when Israel needed a great water supply, God brought water out of rocks (see Exodus 17:6; Numbers 20:11).

18. **THE FOOD OF THEIR FANCY:** Instead of being grateful for God's marvelous provisions of manna, the Israelites complained against God and Moses. God sent them meat but also judged them (see Numbers 11).

19. **PREPARE A TABLE IN THE WILDERNESS:** The answer was "yes," but the question implied a sarcastic lack of faith.

27. **RAINED MEAT:** A poetic description of the quail which dropped into Israel's camp in the wilderness (see Numbers 11:31–35).

41. **LIMITED THE HOLY ONE:** The Israelites did this by doubting God's power.

42. **DID NOT REMEMBER HIS POWER:** The generations of Israelites who left Egypt and eventually died in the wilderness were characterized by ignoring God's previous acts of power and faithfulness. The verses that follow (verses 42–55) rehearse the plagues and miracles of the exodus from Egypt, which demonstrated God's omnipotence and covenant love.

57. **DECEITFUL BOW:** This is a useless bow.

60. **TABERNACLE OF SHILOH:** Shiloh was an early location of Jehovah worship in the Promised Land. The capture and removal of the ark from Shiloh by the Philistines symbolized God's judgment (see Joshua 18:1; 1 Samuel 1:9; 3:1; 4:1–22).

65. **MIGHTY MAN . . . WINE:** The picture is that of a furious, raging warrior entering the battle on Israel's side.

68. **THE TRIBE OF JUDAH:** Instead of the prestigious tribes, God chose Judah. In Judah was Mount Zion, where the central worship center of Jehovah was located. Also, David their king, as well as his royal descendants, were from this tribe.

Read Psalm 82, noting the key words and phrases indicated below.

A PLEA FOR JUSTICE: Psalm 82, like Psalm 2 and Psalm 58, focuses on the injustices of tyranny. The psalmist pictures God standing in the assembly of earthly leaders, to whom He has delegated authority, and condemning their injustices.

82:1. **GOD STANDS:** The structure of this psalm is as follows: (1) the assembly of world leaders before God (verse 1); (2) the evaluation of world leaders by God (verses 2–7); and (3) the replacement of world leaders with God (verse 8). The final prayer of the psalmist in verse 8 is that God Himself will take direct control of this world's affairs.

CONGREGATION OF THE MIGHTY: The scene opens with God having called the world leaders together.

AMONG THE GODS: Some have taken this psalm to be about demons or false pagan gods. The best interpretation is that these gods are human leaders, such as judges, kings, legislators, and presidents (see Exodus 22:8–9, 28; Judges 5:8–9). God, the great Judge, presides over these lesser judges.

2–4. JUDGE UNJUSTLY: God accuses the lesser human judges of social injustices which violate the Mosaic law (e.g., Deuteronomy 24).

5. DARKNESS: This signifies both intellectual ignorance and moral iniquity.

FOUNDATIONS OF THE EARTH ARE UNSTABLE: When leaders rule unjustly, the divinely established moral order that undergirds human existence is undermined.

6. I SAID: Kings and judges are set up, ultimately, by the decree of God (see Psalm 2:6). God, in effect, invests His authority in human leaders for the stability of the universe (see Romans 13:1–7). But God may revoke this authority (see verse 7).

"YOU ARE GODS": Jesus, in quoting this phrase in John 10:34, supported the interpretation that the gods were human beings. In a play on words, He claims that if human leaders can be called gods, certainly the Messiah can be called God.

CHILDREN OF THE MOST HIGH: These were created by God for noble life.

7. DIE LIKE MEN: In spite of being made in God's image, they were mortal and would die like human beings.

FALL LIKE . . . PRINCES: The unjust rulers would become vulnerable to the violent deaths which often accompanied tyranny.

8. YOU SHALL INHERIT ALL NATIONS: The psalmist prayerfully anticipates the future when God will set up His kingdom and restore order and perfect justice to a sin-cursed world (see Psalms 96; 97; Isaiah 11:1–5).

UNLEASHING THE TEXT

1) What can we learn about God from Psalm 73?

_____

_____

_____

_____

_____

_____

2) According to Psalm 75, why is God's judgment an occasion for praise?

_____

_____

_____

_____

_____

3) What is the evidence of God's goodness in Psalm 76?

_____

_____

_____

_____

_____

4) How does Psalm 82 define goodness?

_____

_____

_____

_____

EXPLORING THE MEANING

God's blessings are insurmountable. Psalm 73 is an interesting study of the question that is also found in the book of Job: *Why do the wicked prosper?* The psalmist had evidently wrestled with that question for some time, and he started the song with his conclusion: "Truly God is good to Israel, to such as are pure in heart" (verse 1). After stating that principle, he looked back to his time of struggle. He confessed he "was envious of the boastful, when I saw the prosperity of the wicked" (verse 3). He wondered why the wicked of his day seemed to have such blessed lives in spite of their rebellion against God's will and God's values. He even wondered if he had chosen the wrong path. The turning point for the psalmist's contemplations was an encounter with God in the sanctuary, where he realized the blessings of the wicked were fleeting but serving God offered value for eternity. This realization culminates in one of the loveliest expressions in all of Scripture: "Whom have I in heaven but You? And there is none upon earth that I desire besides You. My flesh and my heart fail; but God is the strength of my heart and my portion forever" (verses 25–26).

God often demonstrates His goodness through judgment. God is good, but we cannot fall into the trap of connecting His goodness exclusively to blessings. It is easy for us to think that God only demonstrates His goodness by bringing blessings and positive circumstances into the lives of His people, but Psalm 75 shows another layer of God's goodness. Specifically, the psalmist praises God's ability and willingness to bring judgment against evil. The psalm begins with an expression of praise: "We give thanks to You, O God, we give thanks! For Your wondrous works declare that Your name is near" (verse 1). But we soon realize that the "wondrous works" under discussion are primarily God's decision to act in judgment against the wicked. Speaking in God's voice, the psalmist declares, "When I choose the proper time, I will judge uprightly" (verse 2), and, "But God is the Judge: He puts down one, and exalts another" (verse 7). It is important to note that these are demonstrations of God's goodness.

God also demonstrates His goodness by withholding judgment. Psalm 78 is a history lesson written to remind the younger generations of God's faithfulness in Israel's history despite the people's continued rebellion. The song focuses mostly on the events after the exodus and during the Israelites' forty years of wandering in the desert. During that time, God's people rejected Him in many ways. "They did not keep the covenant of God," wrote the psalmist. "They refused to walk in His law, and forgot His works and His wonders that He had shown them" (verses 10–11). The crux of the psalm occurs in verses 37–39: "For their heart was not steadfast with Him, nor were they faithful in His covenant. But He, being full of compassion, forgave their iniquity, and did not destroy them. Yes, many a time He turned His anger away, and did not stir up all His wrath; for He remembered that they were but flesh, a breath that passes away and does not come again." The main thrust of the song is God's continued goodness and faithfulness toward His people for generations, despite their continued rebellion against Him. That same goodness and mercy ultimately resulted in Jesus sacrificing Himself on the cross so that the elect's sins would be forgiven and their relationship with Him restored.

REFLECTING ON THE TEXT

5) What is goodness? Who defines it and is the standard by which all other forms of goodness are measured? Why is this important?

_____

_____

_____

_____

_____

6) How does God's goodness relate to His action against evil and injustice?

_____

_____

_____

_____

_____

7) How does God's goodness relate to His mercy in spite of His people's sin?

_____

_____

_____

_____

_____

8) What are other specific ways God demonstrates His goodness to those who follow Him?

_____

_____

_____

_____

_____

PERSONAL RESPONSE

9) What are appropriate ways you can respond even this week to God's goodness demonstrated in your life?

_____

_____

_____

_____

_____

_____

10) What sins in your life are currently hindering you from expressing God's goodness with others?

_____

_____

_____

_____

_____

_____

7

PSALMS OF THE WONDER OF GOD
Psalms 84; 88–89

DRAWING NEAR
Does God captivate your mind, affections, and will so that you are in awe of Him?

_____

_____

_____

_____

_____

_____

_____

_____

_____

THE CONTEXT
In the previous lesson, we reviewed several psalms connected to Asaph that are included in Book III of the Psalms. All of those psalms focused on certain aspects of God's goodness. In this lesson, we will discuss three more songs from Book III, each written by a different author.

The first psalm that we will examine, Psalm 84, is connected to the sons of Korah, whom we discussed in lesson 4 of this study. The second psalm, Psalm 88, was written by a man named "Heman the Ezrahite." The third psalm that we will cover, Psalm 89, was written by an individual known as "Ethan the Ezrahite." The book of 1 Kings gives us a clue about the identities of these men:

"For [Solomon] was wiser than all men—*than Ethan the Ezrahite, and Heman, Chalcol, and Darda, the sons of Mahol; and his fame was in all the surrounding nations*" (4:31, emphasis added). So, Ethan and Heman were likely contemporaries of David and Solomon. They were known for their wisdom and, apparently, both men were also gifted musicians.

Importantly, Psalm 89 is an example of a "messianic psalm"—a psalm that directly foreshadows or points forward to the life and ministry of Jesus, the Messiah. Psalm 89 is considered one of these types of psalms because it points forward to the Messiah's future identity as both a descendant of David (see verses 3–4) and the Son of God (see verses 26–27). There are many other messianic songs present in the Psalter, with Psalm 22 likely being the most prominent because of its detailed and graphic connections to Jesus' crucifixion.

KEYS TO THE TEXT

Read Psalm 84, noting the key words and phrases indicated below.

> THE BLESSEDNESS OF DWELLING IN THE HOUSE OF GOD: *This psalm, like other psalms of ascent (see Psalms 120–134), expresses the joy of a pilgrim traveling up to Jerusalem, then up into the temple to celebrate one of the feasts.*

[INSTRUMENT OF GATH]: The instrument referenced in this title is most probably a guitar-like harp associated with the Gath in Philistia.

84:1. LOVELY IS YOUR TABERNACLE: The temple worship center was lovely because it enabled the Old Testament saint to come into the presence of God (see Psalms 27; 42:1–2; 61:4; 63:1–2). The pilgrim focuses his attention, especially, on the thought of being in the very presence of the Lord God. The New Testament believer-priest, in an even greater way, can come into the presence of the Lord (see Hebrews 4:16; 10:19–22). The structure of this psalm is as follows: (1) the expectation of worshiping God (verses 1–4); (2) the expedition to worship God (verses 5–7); and (3) the elation at worshiping God (verses 8–12).

LORD OF HOSTS: Hosts represent God's angelic armies, thus God's omnipotence over all powers in heaven and on earth (see verses 3, 8, 12).

2. LONGS . . . FAINTS . . . CRY OUT: The psalmist is consumed with his happy but intense desire to worship God in the temple.

3. SPARROW . . . SWALLOW: The psalmist admires these birds who were able to build their nests in the temple courtyards, near the altars of God.

4. BLESSED: This word is used three times (verses 4, 5, 12) to describe the happiness of those who, like the sons of Korah, "lodged all around the house of God" (1 Chronicles 9:27).

6. VALLEY OF BACA: Baca can be translated as "weeping" or "balsam tree." The valley was an arid place on the way to Jerusalem.

THEY MAKE IT A SPRING: The pilgrims traveling to a festival of worship at Jerusalem turn an arid valley into a place of joy.

7. THEY GO FROM STRENGTH TO STRENGTH: The anticipation of joyously worshiping God in Jerusalem overcame the pilgrims' natural weariness in their difficult journey.

9. BEHOLD OUR SHIELD: A metaphor for the king, who also would have participated in a festival at the temple (see Psalm 47:9; Hosea 4:18).

THE FACE OF YOUR ANOINTED: The king is regularly described as God's "anointed" (Psalms 2:2; 18:50; 20:6; 28:8; 89:38, 51). The psalmist thus prays that God would look upon the king with favor, blessing his reign with prosperity.

10. DOORKEEPER: One day standing at the door of the temple, or just being near, was better than a thousand days fellowshipping with the wicked.

11. SUN AND SHIELD: This pictures God's overall provision and protection.

Read Psalms 88–89, noting the key words and phrases indicated below.

A PRAYER FOR HELP IN DESPONDENCY: The author of Psalm 88 writes that he has been ill or injured since the days of his youth and bemoans God's failure to hear his prayer for good health. Yet even though he does not understand God's ways, he does turn to God, thus indicating an underlying trust in the Lord.

[MAHALATH LEANNOTH]: Mahalath is either the name of a tune or an instrument, possibly a reed pipe which was played on sad occasions. Leannoth may mean "to afflict" and describe the despair which permeates this psalm.

[HEMAN THE EZRAHITE]: Heman was a musician from the family of the Kohathites, who founded the Korahite choir (see 1 Chronicles 6:33; 2 Chronicles 5:12; 35:15). He may be the same person who was one of the wise men during

Solomon's reign (see 1 Kings 4:31). Ezrahite may mean "native born," or may be the name of a family clan (see 1 Chronicles 2:6).

88:1. CRIED OUT DAY AND NIGHT: This lament is unusual in that it does not end on a happy note. The psalmist assumes that God is angry with him, but like Job, he knows of no cause for that anger. However, the fact that he turns to God in his distress indicates that he still has faith that the Lord will deliver him. The structure of the psalm is as follows: (1) the psalmist's complaints against God's action (verses 1–9); (2) his challenges to God's wisdom (verses 10–12); and (3) his charges against God's conduct (verses 13–18).

4. GO DOWN TO THE PIT: "Pit" is one of several references to the grave in this psalm (the others include "the dead" in verses 5, 10; "the grave" in verses 3, 5, 11; and the "place of destruction" in verse 11).

5. ADRIFT AMONG THE DEAD: This expresses the idea that death cuts off all ties to friends and family as well as to God.

7. ALL YOUR WAVES: Like the waves rolling on to the seashore, so God has directed trouble after trouble on the psalmist (see verse 17).

8. PUT AWAY MY ACQUAINTANCES: The psalmist claims that the Lord has turned his friends against him. Some see this as a quarantine experience, as from leprosy (see verse 18; also see Job 19:13–20).

9. EYE WASTES AWAY: This could be a description of the psalmist's tears, used as a figure for his collapse under this distress.

10. WONDERS FOR THE DEAD: The psalmist reminds God, through a series of rhetorical questions, that the dead cannot testify to God's goodness.

14. HIDE YOUR FACE: That is, "Why do You not answer my prayers?"

15. DIE FROM MY YOUTH: The psalmist has had some serious illness or injury from the time of his youth.

18. LOVED ONE . . . FRIEND . . . ACQUAINTANCES: See note on verse 8.

REMEMBERING THE COVENANT WITH DAVID, AND SORROW FOR LOST BLESSINGS: Psalm 89 describes the author's attempt to reconcile the seeming contradictions between his theology and the reality of his nation of Israel's conditions.

[ETHAN THE EZRAHITE]: Possibly the Levitical singer who is mentioned in 1 Chronicles 6:42; 15:17, 19.

89:1. I WILL SING OF THE MERCIES: in the initial thirty-seven verses, the psalmist rehearses what he knows to be theologically accurate: God has sovereignly chosen Israel to be His nation and David's descendants to rule. The last third of the psalm reflects the psalmist's chagrin that the nation had been ravaged and the Davidic monarchy had apparently come to a disgraceful end. To his credit, the psalmist refuses to explain away his theology but instead lives with the tension, hopefully to be resolved at a later time with the promised reestablishment of an earthly kingdom under one of David's descendants (see Psalms 110; 132). The structure of the psalm is as follows: (1) God's manifest faithfulness to the Davidic Covenant—God's covenant love (verses 1–4), God's praiseworthiness (verses 5–18), and God's covenant with David (verses 19–37); and (2) God's apparent neglect of the Davidic covenant—the psalmist's lament (verses 38–45), the psalmist's consternation (verses 46–51), the doxology (verse 52).

2. YOU SHALL ESTABLISH . . . HEAVENS: The psalmist exults that the Lord Himself will guarantee the eternality of the Davidic dynasty (see 2 Samuel 23:5).

3. COVENANT WITH MY CHOSEN: The Davidic covenant, culminating in Messiah's reign, was established in 2 Samuel 7 (see 1 Kings 8:23; 1 Chronicles 17; 2 Chronicles 21:7; Psalms 110; 132). The covenant was in the form of a royal grant covenant as God, the great King, chose David as His servant king. In this type of covenant, the person with whom the Lord established the covenant could violate its terms and the Lord would still be obligated to maintain the covenant.

4. SEED . . . FOREVER . . . THRONE: The covenant with David was extended to his descendants. The throne promise guaranteed that the rightful heir to the throne would always be a descendant of David (see verses 29, 36; see also 2 Samuel 7:13, 16, 18; Luke 1:31–33). The genealogies of Jesus qualify Him for the throne (see Matthew 1:1–17; Luke 3:23–38).

5. FAITHFULNESS: The word suggests constant and habitual actions, meaning here that God was reliable. For God to violate this consistency of actions would be to violate His very nature (see verses 1, 2, 8, 24, 33, 49).

6. SONS OF THE MIGHTY: Literally "sons of God," i.e., angels.

7. ASSEMBLY OF THE SAINTS: Literally "holy ones," which pictures a gathering of the angels around their sovereign Lord.

10. RAHAB: A figurative term for Egypt.

12. TABOR AND HERMON: Mountains in Israel pictured joining in praise with the rest of creation.

15. THE JOYFUL SOUND: This refers to a cheer, a shout of joyful homage to God (see Psalms 33:3; 47:5; 95:1; 98:4; 100:1. See also note on Psalm 66:1).

18. SHIELD BELONGS TO THE LORD: The shield was a metaphor for the king (see note on Psalm 84:9).

19. YOUR HOLY ONE: The holy one was the prophet Nathan, whom the Lord used to tell David about His covenant with David (see 2 Samuel 7:4ff.).

25. HAND . . . SEA . . . RIVERS: A reference to the promise of Exodus 23:31 that the Lord would give Israel the land between the Red Sea and the Euphrates River.

27. I WILL MAKE HIM MY FIRSTBORN: The firstborn child was given a place of special honor and a double portion of the inheritance (see Genesis 27; 2 Kings 2:9). However, in a royal grant covenant, a chosen person could be elevated to the level of firstborn sonship and, thus, have title to a perpetual gift involving dynastic succession (see Psalm 2:7). Though not actually the first, Israel was considered the firstborn among nations (see Exodus 4:22); Ephraim, the younger, was treated as the firstborn (see Genesis 48:13–20); and David was the firstborn among kings. In this latter sense of prominent favor, Christ can be called the firstborn over all creation (see Colossians 1:15), in that He is given the preeminence over all created beings as a man. As God, the Son eternally exists and reigns over creation as its Creator.

32. ROD . . . STRIPES: The rod was an instrument for inflicting wounds, and the stripes were the marks left by such a flogging. God's warning reflects His knowledge of the evident potential for disobedience among the descendants of David (see 2 Samuel 7:14). In the lifetime of David's grandsons, for example, the kingdom was split with the ten northern tribes leaving the rulership of the Davidic line (see Jeremiah 31:31; Ezekiel 37:16–17 for the future reunification of the twelve tribes).

33. MY LOVINGKINDNESS I WILL NOT UTTERLY TAKE: Though the Lord might have to discipline David's descendants, He would never remove His covenant from this family (see 2 Samuel 7:15). Thus, the covenant could be conditional in any one or more generations and, yet, be unconditional in its final outcome (see Ezekiel 37:24–28).

37. FAITHFUL WITNESS IN THE SKY: God's covenant with David regarding his descendants was as certain as the establishment of the sun (see verse 36) and the moon in the heavens (see Jeremiah 33:14–26). The promise involved a kingdom "in the earth" (Jeremiah 33:15).

39. RENOUNCED THE COVENANT: The Hebrew word behind "renounced" is rare, and it may better be translated "disdained." It seemed to the psalmist that the condition of Israel indicated that God was neglecting His covenant with David (see Ezekiel 37:1–14).

PROFANED HIS CROWN: This depicts a serious insult to the dynasty because it is of divine origin.

40–45. HEDGES . . . STRONGHOLD . . . PLUNDER . . . SWORD . . . YOUTH: The ruin is depicted in several images: (1) left with broken hedges, thus defenseless; (2) a stronghold whose ruins invite invaders; (3) a weakling plundered by all his enemies; (4) a soldier with a useless sword; and (5) a youth prematurely old.

45. DAYS OF HIS YOUTH . . . SHORTENED: This is a figure for the relative brevity of the Davidic dynasty. The dynasty was cut off in its youth.

46. HIDE YOURSELF FOREVER: By God's seeming refusal to answer prayer and restore the Davidic kingship, it seemed as though God was hiding Himself. Of course, the discipline of disobedient kings had been foretold (see verse 32). According to the prophets, God would eventually restore Israel and the Davidic throne in an earthly kingdom (see Hosea 3:4–5). Never in the Old Testament is there a sense that this Davidic promise would be fulfilled by Christ with a spiritual and heavenly reign.

47. REMEMBER HOW SHORT: The prosperity of the Davidic kingdom is linked to the welfare of all people (see Psalm 72:17; Isaiah 9:7; 11:1–10). If the kingdom fails, who can survive?

49–51. LORD, WHERE ARE YOUR FORMER LOVINGKINDNESSES: Here is a final plea for God to come to the help of His people so they can avoid reproach (see Isaiah 37:17–35).

52. BLESSED BE THE LORD. This blessing, indicating restored confidence, closes not only Psalm 89, but all of Book III of the Psalms.

UNLEASHING THE TEXT

1) What are some of the different blessings listed in Psalm 84? What do these indicate about God?

_____

_____

_____

_____

2) What is the source of Heman's sorrow in Psalm 88?

_____

_____

_____

_____

_____

3) What was Heman seeking from God? Why was he seeking it?

_____

_____

_____

_____

_____

4) In Psalm 89, what elements of God's character does Ethan praise?

_____

_____

_____

_____

_____

EXPLORING THE MEANING

We can find joy in God's presence. Psalm 84 opens with a burst of gladness and expectation: "How lovely is Your tabernacle, O LORD of hosts! My soul longs, yes, even faints for the courts of the LORD; my heart and my flesh cry out for the living God" (verses 1–2). What was the source of this elation? The psalmist was on his way to worship God at the temple. Like children in the backseat of a car, his very soul kept wondering, *Are we there yet? Are we there yet?* He goes on to write, "For a day in Your courts is better than a thousand. I would rather be a doorkeeper in the house of my God than dwell in the tents of wickedness" (verse 10). Note that it was not the temple itself that was the source of the psalmist's expectant joy. Rather, it was the opportunity to spend time in God's presence—to sense the closeness of the Creator and Sustainer of all things. Sometimes, we may forget that we have an incredible opportunity when it comes to God's presence. In Christ, we have ongoing and unlimited access to our heavenly Father. Let us never take such a gift for granted—and let us continually avail ourselves of this wondrous joy!

The wonder of God's presence sustains us even in dark times. As mentioned in this lesson, Psalm 88 is a lament—an outpouring of grief and sorrow. Written by Heman the Ezrahite during a period of intense pain, he cried out to God for both comfort and understanding. Yet there is a key theme woven throughout Heman's writing that reveals an important truth. That theme is present in the beginning of the psalm: "O LORD, God of my salvation, I have cried out day and night before You. Let my prayer come before You; incline Your ear to my cry" (verses 1–2). Later, Heman writes, "LORD, I have called daily upon You; I have stretched out my hands to You" (verse 9), and then again, "But to You I have cried out, O LORD, and in the morning my prayer comes before You" (verse 13). Even during his suffering and grief, Heman had the privilege of spending time in God's presence—and he took advantage of that privilege. He approached God "day and night." He cried out to God "daily" and "in the morning." Even as he tried to understand his affliction, he was sustained by the wondrous and wonderful presence of God.

God alone is worthy of praise. In Psalm 89, Ethan contemplates what feels like a conundrum. God had chosen Israel as His covenant people and promised to bless David's descendants forever. Yet as Ethan looked at his world, he saw Israel divided and David's dynasty in tatters. How could he reconcile those two truths? As he wrestled with these ideas, Ethan began his contemplation on what he knew was solid ground: that God is sovereign and worthy of praise. Like Ethan, we will best deal with the issues of our day when we focus first on the wonder and glory of God and choose to praise Him. God alone is worthy of praise, and we receive strength and steadfastness when we ground ourselves in worship. Incidentally, Ethan never found a resolution in his psalm to his questions about God's sovereignty and the plight of Israel. He left the matter open for future resolution. However, with the benefit of history, we can see the answer to his question today, namely, Jesus Christ. Through Christ, therefore, God has partially fulfilled His promise to Israel and will one day restore them as a nation in the promised land.

REFLECTING ON THE TEXT

5) God is omnipresent, thus He is always present, but how can you orient your mind to dwell on that reality and its implications for you even today?

_____

_____

_____

_____

_____

6) Why should you be in wonder and awe of God? How does that draw you nearer to Him?

_____

_____

_____

_____

_____

7) Why is it critical to commune with God daily?

_____

_____

_____

_____

_____

8) What are specific ways Christians can ground themselves in worshiping God?

_____

_____

_____

_____

_____

PERSONAL RESPONSE

9) What sins have hindered you from spending time with God and enjoying His presence each day?

_____

_____

_____

_____

_____

_____

10) What disciplines or activities best help you to experience God's presence and worship Him? How can you incorporate them more fully into your daily and weekly routines?

_____

_____

_____

_____

_____

_____

8

PSALMS OF GOD'S COMPASSION
Psalms 90–92; 98–99

DRAWING NEAR
What are some examples of God's compassion? How do these stimulate you to worship Him?

_____

_____

_____

_____

_____

_____

_____

_____

_____

_____

_____

THE CONTEXT
In this lesson, we will explore several songs from Book IV of the Psalms, which covers Psalms 90–106. Each of these psalms focus on the theme of God's compassion. In Hebrew, the word translated "compassion" is derived from the Hebrew word for "womb." The term thus conveys the intense feelings that a mother has to love, protect, and nurture her child, as in Isaiah 49:15: "Can a woman forget her nursing child, and not have compassion on the son of her womb?"

But the term also describes the compassion that a father has for his child and, by extension, the compassion that the Heavenly Father has toward His children: "As a father pities his children, so the LORD pities those who fear Him" (Psalm 103:13). The Lord instructed His people to model the compassion that He had shown them in their relationships with one another (see Zechariah 7:9–10). They were to especially have compassion on the poor: "He who has pity on the poor lends to the LORD, and He will pay back what he has given" (Proverbs 19:17).

Many of the psalms included in Book IV are unattributed to specific authors. One notable exception is Psalm 90, which was written by Moses, making it the oldest known song in the Psalter. Jewish tradition also attributes Psalm 91 to Moses, though that is unconfirmed. The authors of the remaining psalms we will explore in this lesson are all unknown.

KEYS TO THE TEXT

Read Psalms 90–92, noting the key words and phrases indicated below.

> *THE ETERNITY OF GOD, AND MAN'S FRAILTY: Moses begins Psalm 90 with a reflection on God's eternality, then expresses his somber thoughts about the sorrows and brevity of life in their relationship to God's anger, and finally concludes with a plea that God would enable His people to live a significant life.*

[MOSES THE MAN OF GOD]: Moses the prophet (see Deuteronomy 18:15–22) was unique in that the Lord knew him "face to face" (see Deuteronomy 34:10–12). "Man of God" (Deuteronomy 33:1) is a technical term used more than seventy times in the Old Testament, always referring to one who spoke for God. It is used of Timothy in the New Testament (see 1 Timothy 6:11; 2 Timothy 3:17).

90:1. LORD: The thrust of this magnificent prayer from Moses is to ask God to have mercy on frail human beings living in a sin-cursed universe. The psalm seems to have been composed as the older generation of Israelites who had left Egypt were dying off in the wilderness (see Numbers 14). The structure of the psalm is as follows: (1) praise of God's eternality (verses 1–2); (2) perception of man's frailty (verses 3–12); and (3) plea for God's mercy (verses 13–17).

OUR DWELLING PLACE: God was Israel's sanctuary for protection, sustenance, and stability (see Deuteronomy 33:27; Psalm 91:9).

2. FROM EVERLASTING TO EVERLASTING: God's nature is without beginning or end, free from all succession of time, and contains in itself the cause of time (see Psalm 102:27; Isaiah 41:4; 1 Corinthians 2:7; Ephesians 1:4; 1 Timothy 6:16; Revelation 1:8).

3. YOU TURN MAN TO DESTRUCTION: The unusual Hebrew word for destruction has the idea of crushed matter. Though different from the dust of Genesis 3:19, this phrase is no doubt a reference to that passage. Humanity lives under a sovereign decree of death and cannot escape it.

4. A WATCH IN THE NIGHT: A watch was a four-hour period of time (see Exodus 14:24; Lamentations 2:19; 2 Peter 3:8).

5. LIKE A FLOOD: Humankind is snatched from the earth as though it were being swept away by floodwaters.

LIKE A SLEEP: Humanity lives its existence as though asleep or in a coma. People are insensitive to the brevity of life and the reality of God's wrath.

7. CONSUMED BY YOUR ANGER: The physical bodies of the human race wear out by the effects of God's judgment on sin in the universe (see Deuteronomy 4:25–28; 11:16–17). Death comes from sin (see Romans 5:12).

8. THE LIGHT OF YOUR COUNTENANCE: All sin is in clear view to the "face" of God.

9. LIKE A SIGH: After struggling through his life of afflictions and troubles, a person's life ends with a moan of woe and weariness.

10. SEVENTY YEARS ... EIGHTY YEARS: Though Moses lived to be 120 years old, and "His eyes were not dim nor his natural vigor diminished" (Deuteronomy 34:7), human life was usually more brief and lived under the anger of God. Because of this certain and speedy end, life is sad.

11. AS THE FEAR OF YOU ... YOUR WRATH: Instead of explaining away life's curses, a wise person will recognize God's wrath toward sin as the ultimate cause of all afflictions and, consequently, learn to fear God.

12. NUMBER OUR DAYS: Evaluate the use of time in light of the brevity of life.

HEART OF WISDOM: Wisdom repudiates autonomy and focuses on the Lord's sovereignty and revelation.

15. GLAD ... AFFLICTED US: A prayer that a person's days of joy would equal his days of distress.

17. THE BEAUTY OF THE LORD: The Lord's beauty implies His delight, approval, and favor.

ESTABLISH THE WORK OF OUR HANDS: By God's mercy and grace, one's life can have value, significance, and meaning (see 1 Corinthians 15:58).

SAFETY OF ABIDING IN THE PRESENCE OF GOD: Psalm 91 describes God's ongoing sovereign protection of His people from the ever-present dangers and terrors which surround humanity.

91:1. HE WHO DWELLS: The original setting of Psalm 91 may be that of an army about to go to battle. Most of the terrors mentioned in this psalm are left undefined, no doubt intentionally, so that no kind of danger is omitted from application. Believers in every age can read this psalm to learn that nothing can harm a child of God unless the Lord permits it. However, in light of the many references in the Psalms to the future messianic kingdom (see especially Psalms 96–100), this psalm must then be read as being literally fulfilled. The psalm is structured as follows: (1) the Lord's protection—the confidence (verses 1–2), the dangers (verses 3–6), the examples (verses 7–13); and (2) the Lord's pledge (verses 14–16).

SECRET PLACE OF THE MOST HIGH: An intimate place of divine protection. The use of "Most High" for God emphasizes that no threat can ever overpower Him.

SHADOW OF THE ALMIGHTY: In a land where the sun can be oppressive and dangerous, a shadow was understood as a metaphor for care and protection.

3. SNARE OF THE FOWLER: A fowler trapped birds. Here, the metaphor represents any plots against the believer intended to endanger his life.

THE PERILOUS PESTILENCE: The reference here and in verse 6 is specifically to dreaded diseases, plagues, and epidemics (see Jeremiah 14:12; Ezekiel 5:12; 14:19).

4. UNDER HIS WINGS: This pictures the protection of a parent bird (see note on Psalm 57:1).

8. ONLY WITH YOUR EYES: The righteous are so safe in disaster all around them that they are only spectators.

11–12. HIS ANGELS: This promise of angelic protection was misquoted by Satan in his temptation of the Messiah (see Matthew 4:6).

13. TREAD . . . LION AND THE COBRA. In general, a metaphor for God's protection from all deadly attacks (see notes on Psalm 58:4ff.).

14. HE HAS SET HIS LOVE UPON ME: God Himself is the speaker in this section (verses 14–16), and He describes the blessing He gives to those who know and love Him. The word for love means a "deep longing" for God, or a "clinging" to God.

16. WITH LONG LIFE I WILL SATISFY HIM: Long life was a specific promise to the Old Testament saint for obedience to the law (e.g., Exodus 20:12; Proverbs 3:2). The prophets also promise it to God's people in the future messianic kingdom (see Isaiah 65:17–23).

PRAISE TO THE LORD FOR HIS LOVE AND FAITHFULNESS: Psalm 92 is an expression of exuberance that God is merciful in salvation, great in His works of creation, just in His dealings with the wicked, and faithful in prospering His children.

[FOR THE SABBATH DAY]: In the postexilic community, some psalms were sung throughout the week in connection with the morning and evening sacrifice; others were designated especially for Sabbath worship.

1. GIVE THANKS TO THE LORD: The structure of this psalm is as follows: (1) an expression of theistic optimism (verses 1–5); (2) an observation concerning righteous sovereignty (verses 6–9); and (3) a testimony to God's goodness (verses 10–15).

2. LOVINGKINDNESS ... FAITHFULNESS: These attributes are constant themes of the Psalms (see notes on Psalms 85:7; 89:5; see also Luke 10:2).

10. MY HORN: See note on Psalm 75:4.

ANOINTED WITH FRESH OIL: This figure is based on a practice of making an animal's horns gleam by rubbing oil on them. Thus God, in effect, had invigorated the psalmist (see Psalms 23:5; 133:2).

11. MY DESIRE ON MY ENEMIES: God granted the psalmist's desire by bringing his enemies to ruin.

12. FLOURISH LIKE A PALM TREE: The palm tree and the cedar symbolized permanence and strength (see verse 14). They are in contrast to the transience of the wicked, who are pictured as temporary as grass (verse 7). See notes on Psalm 1.

13. PLANTED IN THE HOUSE OF THE LORD: A tree planted in the courtyard of the temple symbolized the thriving conditions of those who maintain a close relationship with the Lord. (The simile of a green olive tree is used in the same way in Psalm 52:8.)

Read Psalms 98–99, noting the key words and phrases indicated below.

SONG OF PRAISE TO THE LORD FOR HIS SALVATION AND JUDGMENT: Psalm 98 proclaims the excitement and joy of the earth over the rule of the Lord in the kingdom. This psalm is given over entirely to praise, with only a brief mention of the wicked.

98:1. SING TO THE LORD A NEW SONG: The structure of this psalm is as follows: (1) celebration of the Lord's victorious reign, including triumphs of the Lord (verses 1–3), and praise to the Lord (verses 4–6); and (2) exaltation of the Lord's righteous judgments (98:7–9).

RIGHT HAND . . . HOLY ARM: These are symbols of power.

THE VICTORY: The Lord is often pictured in the Old Testament as a divine Warrior (see Exodus 15:2–3; Psalms 18; 68:1–8; Isaiah 59:15ff.). According to the prophets, Christ will begin His millennial reign following His victory over the nations of the world, which will gather against Israel in the end times (see Zechariah 14:1–15; Revelation 19:11–21).

3. HIS MERCY AND HIS FAITHFULNESS: See note on Psalm 89:5.

SALVATION: These words are a metaphor for the Lord's establishment of His righteous kingdom on earth (see Isaiah 46:13; 51:5–8).

4. SHOUT JOYFULLY: A great cheer which greets and welcomes a king (see Zechariah 9:9; Matthew 21:4–9).

BREAK FORTH: The idea is that of an eruption of praise which could not be contained (see Isaiah 14:7; 44:23; 55:12).

5–6. HARP . . . TRUMPETS . . . HORN: These are instruments normally used in temple worship (see 1 Chronicles 16:5–6; 2 Chronicles 5:12–13; 29:25–30; Ezra 3:10–13).

8. RIVERS CLAP THEIR HANDS: Different parts of nature are pictured as rejoicing in this global scene of joy (see Isaiah 35:1–2; Romans 8:19–21).

PRAISE TO THE LORD FOR HIS HOLINESS: The author of Psalm 99 encourages praise to the king for His holiness, which is the separateness of God's being from all other creatures and things, as well as His moral separateness from sin.

99:1. THE LORD REIGNS: The theme of this psalm can be summed up in its last phrase: "The LORD our God is holy"(verse 9). The psalmist also exults in the truth that such a holy God has had an intimate saving relationship with Israel throughout her history (see verses 6–9). The psalm is structured as follows: (1) exaltation of the King's holiness (verses 1–5); and (2) examples of the King's holiness (99:6–9).

4. KING'S STRENGTH ALSO LOVES JUSTICE: "King's strength" may be a kind of epithet for God; or (combining this phrase with verse 3) the psalmist may be saying that a holy name is the strength of a just king.

EQUITY: i.e., fairness (see Isaiah 11:1–5).

5. HIS FOOTSTOOL: In general, this is a metaphor for the temple in Jerusalem (see Isaiah 60:13; Lamentations 2:1); but more specifically, this is a metaphor for the ark of the covenant (1 Chronicles 28:2). Footstools were included with the thrones of the kings of Israel (see 2 Chronicles 9:18).

6. MOSES . . . AARON . . . SAMUEL: Using three of the nation's famous heroes for examples, the psalmist demonstrates that a holy God has had an enduring, intimate, and saving relationship with Israel.

7. CLOUDY PILLAR: This was a medium of divine direction (see Exodus 13:21–22; 33:9–10; Numbers 12:5; Deuteronomy 31:15ff.).

TESTIMONIES . . . ORDINANCE: Terms used in Psalms for God's Word (see Psalm 119).

9. HIS HOLY HILL: This is the hill in Jerusalem where the temple was built (see Psalms 15:1; 24:3), and where it will be located in the future messianic kingdom (see Isaiah 24:23).

UNLEASHING THE TEXT

1) In Psalm 90, what did Moses communicate about God's compassion?

_____

_____

_____

_____

_____

2) Why does humanity need God's compassion? Why is this element of His character important?

_____

_____

_____

_____

_____

3) How does Psalm 91 communicate the idea of deliverance?

_____

_____

_____

_____

4) How is God's compassion evident in the gospel message of salvation?

_____

_____

_____

_____

_____

EXPLORING THE MEANING

God is eternal and unchanging. Psalm 90 is a prayer of Moses. It was likely expressed and recorded while the Israelites were wandering in the wilderness, which was a stressful and dangerous time for God's people. Moses began his prayer by proclaiming God's eternality and unchanging nature. "Lord, You have been our dwelling place in all generations," he declared. "Before the mountains were brought forth, or ever You had formed the earth and the world, even from everlasting to everlasting, You are God" (verses 1–2). Moses emphasized God's timelessness and compared God's eternal nature with the fleeting lives of humanity: "For all our days have passed away in Your wrath; we finish our years like a sigh" (verse 9). God's eternal nature makes Him entirely unlike anything we have experienced as human beings. He is completely separate from us and far above us. He needs nothing from us and receives nothing from us—yet we are entirely dependent on Him. Incredibly, despite the gulf between us, God deals with us mercifully. As Moses well understood, God treats us with love, which is our only hope.

Without God's compassion, we are lost. In many ways, Moses' prayer in Psalm 90 is a foreshadowing of the gospel. Specifically, Moses understood our inability to deal with our own sin. As Paul wrote in Romans 3:23, "For all have sinned and fall short of the glory of God." Because of this understanding, the final portions of Moses' prayer are laser-focused on God's mercy and compassion. "Have compassion on Your servants," he prayed. "Oh, satisfy us early with Your mercy, that we may rejoice and be glad all our days!" (verses 13–14). His concluding plea is both poignant and passionate: "And let the beauty of the LORD our God be upon us, and establish the work of our hands for us; yes, establish the work of our hands" (verse 17). Scripture makes it clear that we are helpless to solve the problem of our sin. We are dead in our trespasses, and the wages of our sin is death—both physically and spiritually. Like Moses, we must appeal to God's compassion for salvation. Yet the wonderful news of the gospel is that salvation has already been accomplished, and it is applied to those who believe it through repenting of their sin and placing their faith in Christ.

We worship the God-Who-Forgives. Psalm 99 is a brief expression of praise to God for His holiness. Yet there is an interesting moment near the end of the psalm that directly ties to the theme of compassion. The psalmist begins by praising God's greatness and exalting Him because of His justice. He instructs his hearers to praise God's "awesome name" because He is "holy" (verse 3). Then, in verses 6–7, the psalmist looks back to the history of Israel and highlights three leaders who spoke to God as representatives of the people. The next line is key: "You answered them, O LORD our God; You were to them God-Who-Forgives" (verse 8). While it is true that God did punish the Israelites for their constant rebellion, His interactions with all people have been filled with and fueled by compassion. Specifically, the psalmist declared, "You were to them God-Who-Forgives," meaning that forgiveness is an expression of God's character. This is the same God we worship today—the same God, in the Person of the Son, who sacrificed Himself to provide atonement for sin. He is the "God-Who-Forgives."

REFLECTING ON THE TEXT

5) How does God's eternal nature provide blessings and benefits for humanity?

6) How have you yourself been forgiven by God and known His compassion?

7) In Psalm 90, Moses pleaded twice for God to "establish the work of our hands." What does that mean?

8) How would you explain the depth and breadth of God's forgiveness to someone who had never encountered Scripture?

PERSONAL RESPONSE

9) What is an appropriate way for you to respond to God's forgiveness?

_____

_____

_____

_____

_____

_____

_____

10) Where do you currently have an opportunity to speak with others in your life about "God-Who-Forgives"?

_____

_____

_____

_____

_____

_____

_____

9

Psalms of Praise
Psalms 101; 103–104; 106; 109

Drawing Near
Who or what is the object of your praise in your daily life? How can you even more closely align your praise with Scripture's?

_____

_____

_____

_____

_____

_____

_____

_____

_____

_____

_____

_____

_____

_____

The Context
The psalms included in Book IV of the Psalter are 90–106. The psalms included in Book V are 107–150. In this lesson, we will cover a few psalms from each of those books. Among those, we know that Psalms 101, 103, and 109 were written by David, because they are directly attributed to him. Many scholars

believe that Psalm 104 is a continuation of Psalm 103 and was also written by David. The origins of Psalm 106 are unknown, though David is a candidate for its authorship.

The psalms included in this lesson are all centered on praising God. Of course, that theme applies to many of the songs found throughout all five books of the Psalter—praise and worship are primary themes. However, these psalms have a particular goal of leading others to join with the author in exalting God and declaring His praises.

The final psalm in this lesson, Psalm 109, is what scholars often refer to as an "imprecatory psalm." This is a poem or prayer that implores God to call down judgment or destruction on someone who has violated His commands. There are several examples of imprecatory psalms throughout the Psalter. Importantly, the goal is not to curse wrongdoers out of anger or vengeance but to enlist God in the administration of justice.

KEYS TO THE TEXT

Read Psalm 101, noting the key words and phrases indicated below.

> *PROMISED FAITHFULNESS TO THE LORD: Psalm 101 expresses the righteous commitments of the mediatorial king (David) to his eternal king (the Lord) in regard to his own personal life and the lives of those who inhabit the kingdom.*

101:1. I WILL SING OF MERCY AND JUSTICE: Possibly, after David's time, this psalm was used later at the coronations of future kings over Israel. Ultimately, only King Jesus would perfectly fulfill these holy resolutions (see Isaiah 9:6–7; 11:1–5). The structure of this psalm is as follows: (1) personal life of the king (verses 1–4); and (2) personal outcome of kingdom inhabitants—the just (verse 6), and the unjust (verses 5, 7–8).

2. PERFECT WAY: As the king goes, so go his followers (see verse 6).

WHEN WILL YOU COME TO ME: This is not an eschatological expectation but rather a personal expression of David's need for God's immanent involvement in his earthly kingship.

MY HOUSE: The king first starts with his own personal life (verse 7), and then looks beyond to his kingdom (verses 5, 8).

3. MY EYES: The next two verses are similar to the "blessed man" in Psalm 1:1. Here, the king desires to look at nothing but that which is righteous (see verse 6).

4. WICKEDNESS: The king will not engage in wickedness (see verse 8).

5. SLANDERS . . . HAUGHTY LOOK . . . PROUD HEART: Neither character assassination nor pride will be tolerated in the kingdom.

6. THE FAITHFUL OF THE LAND: This group is compared to "the wicked of the land" in verse 8.

7. DECEIT . . . LIES: A premium is put on truth as foundational for a kingdom associated with the God of truth (see John 14:6).

8. THE LAND . . . THE CITY OF THE LORD: Israel and Jerusalem, respectively.

Read Psalms 103–104, noting the key words and phrases indicated below.

PRAISE FOR THE LORD'S MERCIES: Psalms 103 and 104 appear as an intentional pair designed to promote the blessing and exaltation of God. This psalm represents a soliloquy in which David surveys God's goodness and encourages the angels and the works of God's creation to join him in divine praise.

103:1. BLESS THE LORD, O MY SOUL: See Psalms 103:2, 22; 104:1, 35. The structure of this psalm is as follows: (1) a call for human praise—personally (verses 1–5) and corporately (verses 6–19); (2) a call for creation's praise—angels (verses 20–21) and works of creation (verses 22a–b); and (3) a refrain of personal praise (verse 22c).

2. FORGET NOT ALL HIS BENEFITS: These earthly gifts from God included: (1) forgiveness of sin (verse 3), (2) recovery from sickness (see verse 3), (3) deliverance from death (verse 4), (4) abundant lovingkindness and mercy (verse 4), and (5) food to sustain life (verse 5).

3. DISEASES: This is not a promise but a testimony which should be understood in the light of Deuteronomy 32:39.

5. YOUTH IS RENEWED LIKE THE EAGLE'S: The mysterious way of the long-lived eagle symbolized strength and speed (see Exodus 19:4; Jeremiah 48:40), which also characterizes human youth. As a general rule, a person blessed of God will grow weak and slow down less rapidly than otherwise (see Isaiah 40:29–31, which uses the same language).

6–19. THE LORD EXECUTES RIGHTEOUSNESS: The psalmist rehearses the attributes of God with which He blesses the saints.

7–8. HIS WAYS TO MOSES: See Moses' request in Exodus 33:13 and God's answer in Exodus 34:6–7.

9. NOT ALWAYS STRIVE: There will be a final day of accountability, both at death (see Luke 16:19–31) and the Great White Throne (see Revelation 20:11–15). The Genesis flood served as a stark preview of this truth (see Genesis 6:3).

10. NOT DEALT: God's great mercy (see verse 11) and irreversible, complete justification (see verse 12), have redemptively accomplished for believers in Christ, by the death of Christ (see 2 Corinthians 5:21; Philippians 3:9), what they themselves could not do.

13. AS A FATHER: Unlike the pagan gods, who are apathetic or hostile.

14. DUST. Physically speaking, as Adam was created of dust (see Genesis 2:7), so mankind at death decomposes back into dust (see Genesis 3:19).

15–16. HIS DAYS . . . LIKE GRASS: Man's life is short and transitory (see Isaiah 40:8).

17–18. THE MERCY OF THE LORD: Those who appeal to God's mercy by proper fear (verse 17) and obedience (verse 18) will overcome the shortness of physical life with eternal life. Luke 1:50 quotes Psalm 103:17.

19. HIS THRONE IN HEAVEN: From everlasting to everlasting, God has always ruled over all things (see Psalms 11:4; 47:1–9; 148:8–13). This universal kingdom is to be distinguished from God's mediatorial kingdom on earth.

20–21. HIS ANGELS . . . HIS HOSTS: Unfallen, righteous angels who serve God night and day (see Psalm 148:2; Revelation 5:11–13).

22. HIS WORKS: This refers to God's creation, which is also to His praise (see Psalms 148–150; see also 1 Chronicles 29:10–13).

PRAISE TO THE SOVEREIGN LORD FOR HIS CREATION AND
PROVIDENCE: *In vivid poetic detail, the author of Psalm 104
sings of the sovereign Lord's glory in creation.*

104:1. BLESS THE LORD, O MY SOUL: The psalmist begins by recounting the Lord's glory in creation (see Genesis 1; 2; Job 38–41; Psalms 19:1–6; 148:1–6; Proverbs 30:4; Isaiah 40:1–6; John 1:1–3; Romans 1:18–25; Colossians 1:16–17). He refers to the original creation (verse 5) without forgetting the fall of man and the cursed earth (verses 23, 29, 35). He alternates reciting God's greatness by (1) personal praise to the Creator (verses 1–2, 5–9, 20–30), and (2) declaring God's handiwork to his human audience (verses 3–4, 10–19, 31–35). The flow of the psalm loosely follows the order of creation as first reported in Genesis 1:1–31 but closes (in verse 35) with an allusion to the end-time events recorded in Revelation 20–22: (1) the heavens and earth created (verses 1–9); (2) the needs of creatures met (verses 10–18); (3) the sun and moon (verses 19–23); (4) the sea and its inhabitants (verses 24–26); (5) God's providential care (verses 27–30); and (6) benediction to the Creator (verses 31–35).

VERY GREAT: The Creator is greater than His creation. Therefore, the Creator is to be worshiped, not the creation (see Exodus 20:3–4; Romans 1:29).

1–9. LIGHT . . . CHAMBERS IN THE WATERS: This section approximates the first two days of creation (see Genesis 1:1–8).

3. THE WATERS: Refers to the original creation with the waters above the heavens (see Genesis 1:7–8).

4. SPIRITS . . . FLAME OF FIRE: Hebrews 1:7 attributes these characteristics to angels, describing their swiftness and destructiveness as God's instruments of judgment.

5. FOUNDATIONS: See Job 38:4.

6–9. THE DEEP . . . AT YOUR REBUKE THEY FLED: While this might sound like the worldwide flood of Genesis 6–9, it continues to refer to the creation, especially Genesis 1:9–10 regarding the third day of creation.

10–18. THE SPRINGS . . . GRASS . . . VEGETATION: The Creator provides for the basic needs of His creation with water (verses 10–13); vegetation (verse 14); food-producing vines, trees, and grain (verse 15); trees (verses 16–17); and cliffs (verse 18). This corresponds to the third day of creation (see Genesis 1:11–13).

13. UPPER CHAMBERS: This refers to rain clouds.

19–23. MOON FOR SEASONS . . . BEASTS OF THE FOREST . . . MAN: This section corresponds to the fourth day of creation in Genesis 1:14–19. The work period of predators (the night) is contrasted with the work time of humans (the day).

24–26. SEA . . . TEEMING THINGS: This portion corresponds to the fifth day of creation in Genesis 1:20–23.

26. LEVIATHAN: See notes on Psalm 74:14.

27–30. ALL WAIT FOR YOU: All of creation waits on God for His providential care. These verses allude to the sixth day of creation (see Genesis 1:24–31).

30. YOUR SPIRIT: This, most likely, should be translated "Your breath," which corresponds to "the breath of life" in Genesis 2:7.

31–35. MAY THE GLORY OF THE LORD ENDURE: The psalmist closes with a benediction to the Creator in which he prays that the ungodly might no longer spiritually pollute God's universe (verse 35). This prayer anticipates the new heaven and new earth (see Revelation 21–22).

32. TREMBLES ... SMOKE: Earthquakes and fires caused by lightning.

35. SINNERS ... WICKED: God has been merciful to let His fallen human creation live on (see Genesis 3:1–24), but those who bless and praise the Lord desire to see the day (1) sinful people have been abolished from the earth (see Revelation 20:11–15), and (2) the curse of the earth is reversed (see Revelation 22:3).

Read Psalm 106, noting the key words and phrases indicated below.

JOY IN FORGIVENESS OF ISRAEL'S SINS: Psalm 106 rehearses
God's mercy during Israel's history, in spite of Israel's sinfulness.

106:1. HIS MERCY ENDURES FOREVER: Israel had a long history of sinfulness (see Nehemiah 9:1–38; Psalm 78; Isaiah 63:7–64:12; Ezekiel 20:1–44; Acts 7:2–53; 1 Corinthians 10:1–13). The occasion for this psalm is most likely the repentance (verse 6) of post-exilic Jews who had returned to Jerusalem (verses 46–47). Verses 1, 47, 48 seem to be borrowed from 1 Chronicles 16:34–36, which was sung on the occasion of the ark's first being brought to Jerusalem by David (see 2 Samuel 6:12–19; 1 Chronicles 16:1–7). True revival appears to be the psalmist's intention. The structure of the psalm is as follows: (1) the invocation (verses 1–5); (2) the identification with Israel's sins (verses 6); (3) the confession of Israel's sins— during Moses' time (verses 7–33) and from Joshua to Jeremiah (verses 34–46); (4) the plea for salvation (verse 47); and (5) the benediction (verse 48).

1. GOOD ... MERCY: These attributes of God are especially praiseworthy to the psalmist in light of Israel's historical sin pattern (see verses 6–46).

2–3. WHO CAN UTTER ... BLESSED ARE THOSE: Verse 2 asks the question answered in verse 3.

4–5. THE BENEFIT OF YOUR CHOSEN ONES: The psalmist has the benefits of the Abrahamic covenant in mind. He prays here for personal deliverance (verse 4) and, later, for national deliverance (verse 47).

6. WE . . . FATHERS: The psalmist acknowledges the perpetual sinfulness of Israel, including that of his own generation.

7–12. OUR FATHERS IN EGYPT: This section recalls the crossing of the Red Sea during the exodus by the nation, when Pharaoh and his army were in pursuit (see Exodus 14:1–31).

7. RED SEA: See Exodus 13:18.

8. HIS NAME'S SAKE: The glory and reputation of God provide the highest motive for His actions. This frequent Old Testament phrase appears six other places in the Psalms (Psalms 23:3; 25:11; 31:3; 79:9; 109:21; 143:11).

9. HE REBUKED THE RED SEA: This reliable historical account recalls a true supernatural miracle of God (see Exodus 14:21–22), just as He would later provide a way for the nation to cross the Jordan River (see Joshua 3:14–17).

10. SAVED . . . FROM THE HAND: Quoted in Luke 1:71.

11. NOT ONE OF THEM LEFT: As recorded in Exodus 14:28 (see also Psalm 78:53).

Read Psalm 109, noting the key words and phrases indicated below.

PLEA FOR JUDGMENT OF FALSE ACCUSERS: *David responds in Psalm 109 to those who have launched a vicious verbal assault of false accusations against him.*

109:1. DO NOT KEEP SILENT: This imprecatory psalm of David cannot be conclusively connected by the psalm's general details with any particular incident or person in the king's life such as chronicled in 1 and 2 Samuel; 1 Kings; and 1 Chronicles. This psalm is considered messianic in nature, since Acts 1:20 quotes verse 8 in reference to Judas's punishment for betraying Christ (see Psalms 41:9; 69:25). David reverses roles with his enemies by moving from being the accused in man's court to being the accuser/prosecutor before the bar of God. The structure of the psalm is as follows: (1) the plaintiff's plea (verses 1–5); (2) the punishment desired (verses 6–20); (3) the petition for justice (verses 21–29); and (4) the praise of the Judge (verses 30–31).

O GOD OF MY PRAISE: David begins and ends (see verse 30) with praise for the Chief Justice of the universe. At verse 21, David addresses the Judge as "O GOD the Lord" and at verse 26 as "O LORD my God."

2–5. THE MOUTH OF THE WICKED: David's complaint was that the innocent were being accused by the guilty. He asserted that the charges were without cause (see verse 3). While Doeg the Edomite has been identified by some (see 1 Samuel 21; 22; Psalm 52), the most likely candidate would be Saul (see 1 Samuel 18–27). Eight of the fourteen historical superscriptions in other psalms refer to the sufferings of David related to Saul's pursuits for the purpose of killing David (see Psalms 18; 34; 54; 56; 57; 59; 63; 142).

3. THEY HAVE: In verses 2–5, 20, 25, 27–29, David refers to a group of accusers, in contrast to verses 6–19, where an individual is mentioned. Most likely, the individual is the group leader.

6–20. LET AN ACCUSER STAND: The Mosaic law had anticipated false accusations and malicious witnesses (see Deuteronomy 19:16–21) by decreeing that the false accuser was to be given the punishment intended for the accused. It would appear that David had this law in mind here and in verses 26–29. Thus, his imprecations are not malicious maledictions but rather a call for justice according to the law. These severe words have respect not to the penitent but to the impenitent and hard-hearted foes of God and His cause, whose inevitable fate is set.

8. LET ANOTHER TAKE HIS OFFICE: The apostle Peter cited this verse in Acts 1:20 as justification for replacing Judas the betrayer with another apostle.

21–29. YOUR NAME'S SAKE . . . I AM POOR . . . CLOTHED WITH SHAME: David petitioned the court for justice by asking for deliverance for the judge's sake (verse 21) and then for his own sake (verses 22–25). Afterward, he requested that his enemies be rightfully punished (verses 26–29).

30–31. I WILL GREATLY PRAISE THE LORD: David's praise for the divine magistrate (verse 30) was based on his confidence in the compassion and mercy of the judge (verse 31). Second Samuel 22 and Psalm 18 record the general outcome to David's case, which was tried in God's courtroom.

UNLEASHING THE TEXT

1) What were David's promises in Psalm 101?

_____

_____

_____

_____

_____

2) What does it mean to "bless the Lord" as David proclaimed in Psalm 103?

_____

_____

_____

_____

_____

3) What is the psalmist's primary argument in Psalm 104?

_____

_____

_____

_____

4) What is the relationship between David's anger in Psalm 109 and his calls to praise and worship God in previous psalms?

_____

_____

_____

_____

_____

EXPLORING THE MEANING

Praising God includes our actions. David began Psalm 101 by stating his goal: "I will sing of mercy and justice; to You, O Lord, I will sing praises" (verse 1). Praising God is certainly a worthy goal. But the remainder of the psalm focuses on David's actions and attitudes rather than on words of worship. "I will behave wisely in a perfect way," he declared. "I will walk within my house with a perfect heart" (verse 2). Later he added promises such as, "I will set nothing wicked before my eyes; I hate the work of those who fall away; it shall not cling to me" (verse 3). And, "He who works deceit shall not dwell within my house; he who tells lies shall not continue in my presence" (verse 7). David's message was clear: praising God includes more than verbal expressions. David was a master of those verbal expressions, as we see in his other psalms. However, Psalm 101 is David's declared intention to praise God through his actions. His decisions and attitudes each day would serve as an offering of worship.

Praising God should be specific rather than vague. Psalm 103 is a beautiful expression of worship, and it is bookended by two wonderful injunctions of praise. "Bless the LORD, O my soul," David proclaimed to begin this psalm, "and all that is within me, bless His holy name!" (verse 1). "Bless the LORD, all His works," David proclaimed to end this psalm, "In all places of His dominion. Bless the LORD, O my soul!" (verse 22). In between those two declarations, David took care to be specific in his praise. For example, he extolled the way God "forgives all your iniquities" and "heals all your diseases" (verse 3). He praised God's character: "The LORD is merciful and gracious, slow to anger, and abounding in mercy" (verse 8). If we are not careful, we can drift into generalities when we do remember to verbally express praise and worship to God. "Father, we praise You . . . Lord God, you are worthy of praise . . . " and so on. Such expressions are not wrong, yet we will do better to emulate David in identifying specific, thoughtful avenues for expressing our praise and appreciation of the Most High.

Praising God should include our voices and our words. In addition to praising God through his actions and attitudes, David was intentional about verbalizing his worship. And we should be thankful for it. As we have seen, David's expressions of praise are some of the most lyrical and memorable ever recorded. It is important that we follow the example of David and the other psalmists by intentionally and actively praising God with our voices and our words. "I will sing to the LORD as long as I live," wrote one psalmist. "I will sing praise to my God while I have my being. May my meditation be sweet to Him; I will be glad in the LORD" (104:33–34). "Oh, give thanks to the LORD, for He is good!" declared another psalmist. "For His mercy endures forever. Who can utter the mighty acts of the LORD? Who can declare all His praise?" (106:1–2). Sometimes we are content with reading psalms or other words in praise of God. Sometimes we think thoughts of praise or appreciation to God—and certainly He does hear them. However, there is power in raising our voices to worship God, the Lord Almighty. There is also power in gathering corporately to praise His name and proclaim His glory throughout the nations.

REFLECTING ON THE TEXT

5) What are some actions or attitudes that reflect praise and appreciation to God? Why is He worthy of praise?

_____

_____

_____

_____

_____

_____

6) Why is it often easy for Christians to drift into cliches during times of prayer and praise?

_____

_____

_____

_____

7) What are some specific ways to prevent that kind of drift?

_____

_____

_____

_____

_____

8) David and the other psalmists lived in a culture that was largely illiterate, which is one reason psalms and songs were popular. Why is verbal praise still important today?

_____

_____

_____

_____

_____

PERSONAL RESPONSE

9) Being specific in our worship requires forethought. For that reason, how can you build time into your regular routine to identify specific areas for praising God?

_____

_____

_____

_____

_____

_____

_____

10) What are three ways you can actively, intentionally verbalize your worship of God today?

_____

_____

_____

_____

_____

_____

_____

_____

10

PSALMS OF ASCENT
Psalms 120–123; 126–128; 132

DRAWING NEAR
How do you orient your mind, affections, and will toward worshiping God?

_____

_____

_____

_____

_____

_____

_____

_____

_____

_____

_____

_____

THE CONTEXT
In the previous lessons of this study, we have explored different groupings of psalms that are connected either due to a common author (such as David) or a common theme (such as comfort, repentance, praise, and the like). In this lesson, we will look at a group of psalms joined together by a common journey. They are Psalms 120–134—the "Songs of Ascent."

The Songs of Ascent were hymns that many scholars believe the Jewish pilgrims sang as they climbed their way up the path to Jerusalem (about 2,700 feet in elevation) during three prescribed festivals each year. These feasts included: (1) The Feast of Unleavened Bread (see Leviticus 23:4–8); (2) The Feast of Weeks (also known as Pentecost; see Leviticus 23:15–22); and (3) The Feast of Tabernacles (see Leviticus 23:33–43). All Jewish males were required to travel to Jerusalem each year to attend these three "solemn feasts" (see Exodus 23:14–14; 34:22–23; Deuteronomy 16:16). Biblical scholars believe that the Songs of Ascent were designed to build excitement as the pilgrims grew closer to Jerusalem and to God's temple.

David authored four of these songs (Psalms 122; 124; 131; 133), Solomon wrote one (Psalm 127), and the remaining ten are anonymous. It is not known when these psalms were first collected together. It appears that these songs began far away from Jerusalem (see the references to the cities of Meshech and Kedar, located in Asia Minor and Arabia respectively, in Psalm 120:5) and progressively moved toward Jerusalem until the pilgrims actually reached the temple and finished their worship (see Psalm 134:1–2).

KEYS TO THE TEXT

Read Psalms 120–123, noting the key words and phrases indicated below.

> PLEA FOR RELIEF FROM BITTER FOES: *The author of Psalm 120 and his circumstances are unknown, although it seems as if the worshiper lived at a distance from Jerusalem among unbelieving people.*

120:1. HE HEARD ME: This psalm is broken into three parts: (1) petition (verses 1–2); (2) indictment (verses 3–4); and (3) lament (verses 5–7).

2. FROM LYING LIPS . . . A DECEITFUL TONGUE: See Psalms 52:2–4; 109:2; Romans 3:9–18.

4. SHARP ARROWS . . . COALS: Lies and false accusations are likened to (1) the pain/injury inflicted in battle by arrows, and (2) the pain of being burned with charcoal made from the wood of a broom tree (a desert bush that grows ten to fifteen feet high).

5–7. MY SOUL HAS DWELT TOO LONG: The psalmist actually lives among pagans who do not embrace his desire for peace.

5. MESHECH . . . KEDAR: As previously noted, these cities were located in Asia Minor (see Genesis 10:2) and Arabia (Isaiah 21:16), respectively.

GOD THE HELP OF THOSE WHO SEEK HIM: The author and circumstances of Psalm 121 are unknown. The song strikes a strong note of assurance in four stages that God is help and protection to keep both Israel and individual believers safe from harm.

121:1. I WILL LIFT UP MY EYES: The four stages of this psalm are as follows: (1) God as helper (verses 1–2); (2) God as keeper (verses 3–4); (3) God as protector (verses 5–6); and (4) God as preserver (verses 78).

HILLS: Most likely those in the distance as the pilgrim looks to Jerusalem, especially the temple.

2. MY HELP: The psalmist does not look to the creation but rather the Creator for His help.

3. BE MOVED: See Psalm 37:23–24.

3–4 SLUMBER: The appearance of sleep, see Psalm 44:23. The living God is totally unlike the pagan gods/dead idols (see 1 Kings 18:27).

5. YOUR RIGHT HAND: This represents the place of human need.

6. BY DAY . . . BY NIGHT: Around-the-clock protection is in view.

7–8. ALL EVIL . . . FOREVERMORE: While this seems to have a temporal sense at first glance, there are indications that it looks beyond to eternal life.

THE JOY OF GOING TO THE HOUSE OF THE LORD: In Psalm 122, David expresses his great joy over Jerusalem, which he had settled by defeating the Jebusites and bringing the tabernacle and ark for permanent residency (see 2 Samuel 5–6).

122:1. I WAS GLAD WHEN THEY SAID TO ME: David's desire/prayer was temporarily fulfilled during his son Solomon's reign (see 1 Kings 4:24–25). It is ironic that Jerusalem, which means "city of peace," has been fought over throughout history more than any other city in the world. Prophetically, David's desire will not be experienced in its fullness until the Prince of Peace (see Isaiah 9:6) comes to rule permanently (see Zechariah 14:9, 11) as the promised Davidic King (see 2 Samuel 7:12–13, 16; Ezekiel 37:24–28). The structure of the psalm is as follows: (1) joy over worship (verses 1–5); and (2) prayer over Jerusalem (verses 6–9).

THE HOUSE OF THE LORD: A term used of the tabernacle (see Exodus 23:19; 34:26; 2 Samuel 12:20), not the temple that would be built later by Solomon.

2. STANDING WITHIN YOUR GATES: This occurred sometime after the tabernacle and ark of the covenant had arrived in the city of David (2 Samuel 6). David's joy is that the ark has found its proper location.

3. COMPACT TOGETHER: The Jerusalem of David's day (Zion) was smaller than the enlargement by Solomon.

4. THE TESTIMONY OF ISRAEL: This refers to God's command to go up to Jerusalem three times annually.

6–9. PRAY FOR THE PEACE OF JERUSALEM: A most appropriate prayer for a city whose name means peace and is the residency of the God of peace (see Isaiah 9:6; Romans 15:33; Hebrews 13:20). Compare prayers for the peace of Israel (see Psalms 125:5; 128:6) and other psalms which exalt Jerusalem (see Psalms 128; 132; 147). History would prove that bad times had to come (see Psalms 79; 137) before the best of times (see Revelation 21–22).

PRAYER FOR RELIEF FROM CONTEMPT: *The author of Psalm 123 and the situation that caused him to write this prayer for relief are unknown.*

123:1. UNTO YOU I LIFT UP MY EYES: The psalmist wrote this prayer in two parts: (1) exalting God (verses 1–2); and (2) enlisting God's mercy (verses 3–4). Note the progression of "lifting one's eyes" from Psalm 121:1.

DWELL IN ... HEAVENS: See Psalms 11:4; 103:19; 113:5.

2. SERVANTS ... MASTERS: The psalmist reasons from the lesser to the greater (human to the divine; earthly to the heavenly). One's eyes should be on the Lord to mercifully meet one's needs.

3–4. CONTEMPT ... SCORN: This came from unbelieving pagans, perhaps the Samaritans (see Nehemiah 1:3; 2:19).

Read Psalms 126–128, noting the key words and phrases indicated below.

A JOYFUL RETURN TO ZION: *The author and occasion behind Psalm 126 are again unknown. It is similar to Psalm 85, which rejoices over*

*Israel's return from Egypt, but contrasts with Psalm 137, which
laments the pain of the Babylonian captivity.*

126:1. THE LORD BROUGHT BACK: The author and the occasion of this
psalm are not known, but verse 1 points to a time of return from captivity. Most
likely, this refers to the Babylonian captivity, from which there were three separate returns: (1) under Zerubbabel in Ezra 1–6 (c. 538 BC); (2) under Ezra
in Ezra 7–10 (c. 458 BC); and (3) under Nehemiah in Nehemiah 1–2 (c. 445 BC).
The occasion could be (1) when the foundation for the second temple had been
laid (see Ezra 3:8–10), or (2) when the Feast of Tabernacles was reinstated (see
Nehemiah 8:13–14). The structure of the psalm is as follows: (1) the testimony
of restoration (verses 1–3); (2) prayer for riches (verse 4); (3) wisdom of righteousness (verses 5–6).

THOSE WHO DREAM: The actual experience of liberation, so unexpected,
seemed more like a dream than reality.

2–3. THE LORD HAS DONE: This was first recognized by the surrounding
nations (verse 2) and then the returning remnant (verse 3).

4. BRING BACK: A prayer to restore the nation's fortunes at their best.

STREAMS IN THE SOUTH: The arid region south of Beersheba (called the
Negev), which is utterly dry in the summer but whose streams quickly fill and
flood with the rains of spring. In this manner, the psalmist prays that Israel's fortunes will rapidly change from nothing to everything.

5–6. SOW . . . REAP: By sowing tears of repentance over sin, the nation reaped
the harvest of a joyful return to the land of Israel.

*LABORING AND PROSPERING WITH THE LORD: Solomon is the
author of Psalm 127, but the occasion is unknown. He writes of
God being central in all aspects of life.*

127:1. UNLESS THE LORD BUILDS THE HOUSE: The major message of God
being central to and sovereign in life sounds much like portions of Solomon's Ecclesiastes (see Ecclesiastes 2:24–25; 5:18–20; 7:13–14; 9:1). Psalms 112
and 128 also develop a strong message on the family. God's sovereignty is seen
in three realms: (1) building a house; (2) protecting a city; and (3) earning a living. In all three instances, the sovereign intention of God is far more crucial

to the outcome than man's efforts. Otherwise, a person's endeavor is in vain (see Ecclesiastes 1:2; 12:8).

2. THE BREAD OF SORROWS: Food earned with painful labor.

3–5. CHILDREN: The same principle of God's sovereignty applies to raising a family.

3. HERITAGE . . . REWARD: Children are a blessing from the Lord. There are overtones of God's promise to Abraham to make his offspring like the dust of the earth and stars of heaven (see Genesis 13:16; 15:5).

4–5. LIKE ARROWS . . . QUIVER FULL OF THEM: As arrows are indispensable for a warrior to succeed in battle, so children are invaluable as defenders of their father and mother in time of war or litigation. The more such defenders, the better.

> BLESSINGS OF THOSE WHO FEAR THE LORD: *The author of Psalm*
> *128 and the occasion that caused him to write this song extolling*
> *the blessings of fearing the Lord are unknown. Psalms 112 and 127*
> *also address themes regarding the home.*

128:1. BLESSED IS EVERY ONE: The structure of this psalm is as follows: (1) the basics of fearing the Lord (verses 1, 4); and (2) the blessings of fearing the Lord, both in the present (verses 2–3) and in the future (verses 5–6).

WHO FEARS THE LORD: Psalm 112:1–6 also develops this theme. A good working definition is provided by the parallel line, "who walks in His ways." Fathers (see Psalm 128:1, 4), mothers (see Proverbs 31:30), and children (see Psalm 34:11) are to fear the Lord. This psalm may have been the basis for Jesus' illustration of the two builders (see Matthew 7:24–27).

2–3. YOU SHALL BE . . . IT SHALL BE: Four blessings are recounted: (1) provisions, (2) prosperity, (3) reproducing partner, and (4) flourishing progeny.

3. OLIVE PLANTS. Shoots grow off the main root of an olive tree to reproduce.

5–6. BLESS YOU . . . GOOD OF JERUSALEM: Two realms of blessing are mentioned: (1) personal blessing and (2) national blessing.

6. YES, MAY YOU SEE YOUR CHILDREN'S CHILDREN: See Psalms 103:17; 112:2; Proverbs 13:22; 17:6 on grandchildren. This prayer is for the prosperity of God's people.

Read Psalm 132, noting the key words and phrases indicated below.

> THE ETERNAL DWELLING OF GOD IN ZION: *Essentially, Psalm 132 contains the nation's prayers for David's royal descendants that look ahead, even to the Messiah.*

132:1. LORD, REMEMBER DAVID: The author and occasion are not mentioned. However, the bringing of the tabernacle to Jerusalem in David's time seems likely (compare 2 Samuel 6:12–19 to Psalm 132:6–9). Further, Solomon's quote of verses 8–10 in his dedication of the temple (see 2 Chronicles 6:41–42) makes that time probable. Psalm 132 has strong historical implications with regard to the Davidic covenant (see 2 Samuel 7:10–14; 16; Psalms 89; 132:10–11) plus pronounced messianic and millennial overtones (Psalm 132:12–18). The structure of the psalm is as follows: (1) Israel's first prayer (verse 1); (2) David's vow to God (verses 2–9); (3) Israel's second prayer (verse 10); (4) God's vow to David (verses 11–18).

HIS AFFLICTIONS: This seems to be inclusive from the times of being pursued by Saul (see 1 Samuel 18–26) through God's judgment because David numbered the people (see 2 Samuel 24). Perhaps it focuses on David's greatest affliction, which came from not having the ark in Jerusalem.

1–9. HE SWORE TO THE LORD: This section focuses on David fulfilling his vow to God to bring the tabernacle to rest in Jerusalem and, thus, his descendants are to be remembered by the Lord.

2. THE MIGHTY ONE OF JACOB. A title last used by Jacob in Genesis 49:24.

2–5. UNTIL I FIND A PLACE FOR THE LORD: Although this specific vow is not recorded elsewhere in Scripture, the historical circumstances can be found in 2 Samuel 6; 1 Chronicles 13–16.

6. HEARD OF IT IN EPHRATHAH: This probably refers to David's younger days in Ephrathah, which was an earlier name for Bethlehem (see Ruth 1:1, 2; 4:11), when he and his family had heard of the ark but had not seen it.

6–9. FOUND IT IN THE FIELDS OF THE WOODS: After the ark of the covenant was returned by the Philistines in the days of Saul (see 1 Samuel 7:1–2), it rested at the house of Abinadab in Kirjath Jearim until David decided to move it to Jerusalem (see 2 Samuel 6; 1 Chronicles 13–16).

7. WORSHIP AT HIS FOOTSTOOL: God's throne is in heaven (see Isaiah 66:1) and His footstool is on earth (see Psalm 99:5), figuratively speaking. Thus

to worship at the ark of the covenant on earth would be, so to speak, worshiping at God's footstool.

8. ARISE, O LORD: Since the Holy Place contained the bread of the presence (see Exodus 25:30; 1 Samuel 21:6), the psalmist refers to moving the ark to Jerusalem.

9. LET YOUR PRIESTS BE CLOTHED WITH RIGHTEOUSNESS: This describes the proper inward attire for the priests who would oversee the move.

10–18. FOR YOUR SERVANT DAVID'S SAKE: A prayer that God's promise and favor would not be withheld from David's descendants on the throne of Judah. This section focuses on God's fulfilling His vow to David to perpetuate the Davidic throne and, thus, his descendants are to be remembered by the Lord.

10. YOUR ANOINTED: As David had been anointed king (see 1 Samuel 16:13), so a greater King had been anointed, namely Christ, but not yet seated on the throne (see Isaiah 61:1; Luke 4:18–19).

11–12. THE LORD HAS SOWN IN TRUTH TO DAVID: God's covenant with David (see 2 Samuel 23:5) is summarized here from 2 Samuel 7:11–16 and 1 Kings 9:1–9.

12. IF YOUR SONS WILL KEEP MY COVENANT: This conditional aspect could interrupt the occupation of the throne, but it would not invalidate God's promise to seat forever the Messiah as king one day in the future (see Ezekiel 37:24–28).

13–18. FOR THE LORD HAS CHOSEN ZION: Zion refers to earthly Jerusalem. Yet this section looks forward prophetically to the day when Jesus Christ, the son of David and the son of Abraham (see Matthew 1:1), will be installed by God on the throne of David in the city of God to rule and bring peace on earth, especially Israel (see Psalms 2; 89; 110; Isaiah 25; 26; Jeremiah 23:5, 6; 33:14–18; Ezekiel 37; Daniel 2:44, 45; Zechariah 14:1–11).

UNLEASHING THE TEXT

1) What are some common themes throughout the Songs of Ascent?

_____

_____

_____

_____

_____

2) What places and geographical features are included in these psalms?

_____

_____

_____

_____

_____

3) Solomon wrote Psalm 127. What is the meaning of that song?

_____

_____

_____

_____

_____

4) What does Psalm 132 communicate about the temple in Zion?

_____

_____

_____

_____

_____

EXPLORING THE MEANING

We can cry out to God for protection. The Songs of Ascent were originally written to be sung or recited by travelers on their way to Jerusalem. In the ancient world, any kind of long journey was perilous—not only because of frequent ambushes and robberies but also because of the long distances and financial burdens imposed by travel. It is perhaps because of these considerations that the Songs of Ascent begin with a cry for protection: "In my distress I cried to the LORD, and He heard me. Deliver my soul, O LORD, from lying lips and from a deceitful tongue" (Psalm 120:1–2). The immediate cause for this cry seems to be the original psalmist's pagan neighbors, who did not share his righteous values nor his desire for peace. Subsequent travelers would have taken up that cry to express their desire for protection as they journeyed out of foreign lands and made their way toward God's temple. Psalm 121 echoes this desire for protection but places the focus on the One who provides it: "I will lift up my eyes to the hills—from whence comes my help? My help comes from the LORD" (verses 1–2). As Christians, we also live in a world today that does not always value what God values. Therefore, it is appropriate—even necessary—for us to seek protection and support from our Heavenly Father.

God is able to answer our cry for protection. As we seek God's protection, it is critical that we remember *and believe* that He can provide it. Doubt, fear, and resignation are sins that burden our souls when we are in the midst of trouble—especially when we don't see immediate relief or instant answers on the horizon. This is why the psalmists were intentional about describing God's ability to protect His people: "He will not allow your foot to be moved; He who keeps you will not slumber. Behold, He who keeps Israel shall neither slumber nor sleep" (121:3–4). "'If it had not been the LORD who was on our side,' let Israel now say—'If it had not been the LORD who was on our side, when men rose up against us, then they would have swallowed us alive, when their wrath was kindled against us'" (124:1–3). "Our help is in the name of the LORD, who made heaven and earth" (124:8). Crying out to God for protection is critical in this life. But it is also necessary for us to cry out in faith.

God is sovereign over all areas of life. God's sovereignty is a major theme in Scripture, and especially within the Songs of Ascent. As pilgrims journeyed toward God's city and God's house on Mount Zion, they regularly reminded themselves that God alone was in control of all things. Solomon focused on that theme in Psalm 127, exploring it from three different angles. First, he described God's sovereignty using the imagery of building a home (verse 1). Second, he used the imagery of protecting a city (verse 1). Third, he highlighted God's sovereignty in connection with a critical area of human existence: raising children (verse 3). Bearing children was an especially important responsibility for the Israelites because of God's promise that Abraham's descendants would become a great nation and bless the entire earth (see Genesis 12:1–3). Yet Solomon reminded his people that it was God Himself who had sovereign charge, even over the opening and closing of the womb. Today, our culture pushes us to be self-empowered and independent, striving to achieve our goal in our own strength. Yet all of our effort will be in vain if we fail to remember God's sovereign plan and purpose, and if we fail to bend our efforts toward His will.

REFLECTING ON THE TEXT

5) Do you find it easy or difficult to ask God for help?

6) What are some ways God has revealed His ability to support and protect you in the past?

7) How would you describe God's sovereignty to someone who had never heard about it?

8) What are practical ways to simultaneously work hard and at the same time acknowledge God's sovereignty?

PERSONAL RESPONSE

9) Where do you need protection in your life right now? How can you approach God with that need?

_____

_____

_____

_____

_____

_____

10) What is a specific step you can take this week to acknowledge God's sovereignty over your life? Over the workings of the world?

_____

_____

_____

_____

_____

_____

11

PSALMS OF INTROSPECTION
Psalms 138–145

DRAWING NEAR

Why is it important to examine your heart? Why is it important to reflect on truths about God?

_____

_____

_____

_____

_____

_____

_____

_____

_____

_____

_____

THE CONTEXT

We have noted previously that David is the most prolific author within the Psalter, having written at least seventy-three of the 150 psalms compiled in that volume. However, it is important to note that David experienced tremendous changes in his personal circumstances throughout the entirety of his life. He began writing psalms as a young man and as a shepherd, with plenty of time to contemplate and compose. But later, he wrote his songs while on the run from King

Saul, who sought to murder him on many occasions. And later still, David wrote as a king, recording his perspective as the most powerful person in the region.

Many of David's psalms were written as corporate expressions of worship. This means that they were intended to be shared and sung by many people who had joined together to praise the God of Israel. Yet because of David's unique circumstances, many of his psalms were written as deeply personal, deeply introspective, reflections only between himself and God.

In this lesson, we will explore the final eight psalms attributed to David—Psalms 138–145. As you read, you will feel the power and depth of those moments when David stepped away from everything in his life to contemplate his own thoughts, his own needs, and his own understanding of God.

Keys to the Text

Read Psalms 138–145, noting the key words and phrases indicated below.

> THE LORD'S GOODNESS TO THE FAITHFUL: *The occasion that prompted David's writing of Psalm 138 is unknown, though he might have written it in response to the Davidic covenant (see 2 Samuel 7:12–14, 16).*

138:1. I WILL PRAISE YOU: The structure of this psalm is as follows: (1) individual praise (verses 1–3); (2) international praise (verses 4–5); and (3) invincible praise (verses 6–8).

THE GODS: This can refer to either pagan royalty (see Psalm 82:1) and/ or to the idols they worship.

2. HOLY TEMPLE: This refers to the Mosaic tabernacle, since Solomon's temple had not yet been built.

YOUR WORD ABOVE . . . YOUR NAME: Most likely, this means that God's latest revelation ("Your word") exceeded all previous revelation about God. This would be in concert with David's prayer in 2 Samuel 7:18–29 after he received the Davidic promise (see 2 Samuel 7:12–14, 16).

4. ALL THE KINGS: This is in contrast to Psalm 2:1–3. See Psalms 68:32; 72:11, 12; 96:1, 3, 7, 8; 97:1; 98:4; 100:1; 102:15; 148:11.

6–7. THE LOWLY . . . THE PROUD: David sees himself as "the lowly" and his enemies as "the proud."

8. PERFECT: This refers to God's completed work in David's life, especially the Davidic covenant (see 2 Samuel 7:12–14, 16).

GOD'S PERFECT KNOWLEDGE OF MAN: *Psalm 139 is an intensely personal psalm written by King David in which he expresses his awe that God knew him down to even to the minutest detail.*

139:1. YOU HAVE SEARCHED ME: While the exact occasion for the writing of this psalm is unknown, it is clear David was in awe that God knew everything about him. He might have remembered the Lord's words, "the LORD looks at the heart" (1 Samuel 16:7). The structure of the psalm is as follows: (1) God's omniscience (verses 1–6); (2) God's omnipresence (verses 7–12); (3) God's omnipotence (verses 13–18); and (4) David's obeisance (verses 19–24).

AND KNOWN ME: As it has been in David's life, he prays later (see verses 23–24) that it will continue to be so. David understands that nothing inside him can be hidden from God.

5. HEDGED ME: God used circumstances to limit David's actions.

6. TOO WONDERFUL: See Psalm 131:1; Romans 11:33–36.

7–12. WHERE CAN I GO: God was always watching over David, and thus it was impossible to do anything before which God is not a spectator.

YOUR SPIRIT: A reference to the Holy Spirit (see Psalms 51:11; 143:10).

9. THE WINGS OF THE MORNING: In conjunction with "the uttermost parts of the sea," David uses this literary figure to express distance.

13–18. FORMED . . . COVERED: God's power is magnified in the development of human life before birth. By virtue of the divinely designed period of pregnancy, God providentially watches over the development of the child while still in the mother's womb.

15. SECRET . . . LOWEST PARTS: This language is used figuratively of the womb.

16. YOUR BOOK: This likens God's mind to a book of remembrance.

NONE OF THEM: God ordained David's life before he was conceived.

17–18. HOW PRECIOUS ALSO ARE YOUR THOUGHTS TO ME: David expresses his amazement at the infinite mind of God compared to the limited mind of man, especially as it relates to the physiology of human life (see verses 13–16).

22. PERFECT HATRED: David has no other response to God's enemies than hatred; i.e., he is not neutral toward them, nor will he ever ally himself with them.

23–24. ANY WICKED WAY: In light of verses 19–22, David invites God to continue searching his heart to root out any unrighteousness, even when it is expressed against God's enemies.

24. WAY EVERLASTING: David expresses his desire/expectation of eternal life.

PRAYER FOR DELIVERANCE FROM EVIL MEN: Davidic authorship of Psalm 140 is stated, but the circumstances are unknown. This is like the earlier psalms in the Psalter that feature the usual complaint, prayer, and confident hope of relief.

140:1. DELIVER ME, O LORD: The emphasis here is deliverance from evil plans. The structure of the psalm is as follows: (1) concerning David—"deliver me" (verses 1–3) and "protect me" (verses 4–5); (2) concerning David's enemies—"thwart them" (verses 6–8) and "punish them" (verses 9–11); and (3) concerning the Lord (verses 12–13).

3. ASPS: A type of snake (see Romans 3:13), signifying cunning and venom.

4–5. VIOLENT MEN: The emphasis here is protection from being captured.

6–8. DO NOT GRANT: The emphasis here is on God's thwarting the plans of David's enemy.

7. COVERED MY HEAD: God has figuratively been David's helmet in battle.

9–11. THOSE WHO SURROUND ME: The emphasis here is on God's turning these men's evil plans back on them in judgment.

12–13. I KNOW THAT THE LORD WILL MAINTAIN: David expresses unshakeable confidence in the character of God and the outcome for the righteous (see Psalms 10:17–18; 74:21; 82:3–4).

PRAYER FOR SAFEKEEPING FROM WICKEDNESS: Psalm 141 is another song of lament authored by David for which the occasion of the writing is unknown. This psalm is comprised of four prayers that have been combined into one.

141:1. LORD, I CRY OUT TO YOU: The four prayers that David combines in this psalm are as follows: (1) a prayer for God's haste (verses 1–2); a prayer for personal righteousness (verses 3–5); (3) a prayer for justice (verses 6–7); and (4) a prayer for deliverance (verses 8–10).

2. INCENSE . . . EVENING SACRIFICE: David desired that his prayers and stretching forth for God's help (see Psalms 68:31; 77:2) be as disciplined and regular as the offering of incense (see Exodus 30:7–8) and burnt offerings (see Exodus 29:38–39) in the tabernacle.

3–4. SET A GUARD, O LORD: David prayed that God would protect him from the kind of evil that characterized his own enemy.

5. LET THE RIGHTEOUS STRIKE ME: David acknowledged that God would use other righteous people to answer his prayer in verses 3–4 (see Proverbs 9:8; 19:25; 27:6; 27:17).

6. JUDGES . . . OVERTHROWN: That the leaders of the wicked would be punished by being thrown over a cliff (see Luke 4:28–29) is at the heart of David's prayer (see verse 5).

WORDS . . . SWEET: This is written in the sense that David's words were true.

7. OUR BONES: The basis on which the judges were thrown over the cliff is that they had first done this to the righteous (see verse 10).

10. FALL INTO THEIR OWN NETS: David prays that the wicked will be destroyed by their own devices.

A PLEA FOR RELIEF FROM PERSECUTORS: David wrote Psalm 142 (according to the superscription) under the same circumstances as Psalm 57—during his desperate days hiding in the cave of Adullam as King Saul sought to take his life.

[HE WAS IN THE CAVE]: The account of David hiding in the cave of Adullam is found in 1 Samuel 22:1, within the broader story of King Saul seeking to take his life (see 1 Samuel 18–24).

142:2. I POUR OUT MY COMPLAINT: It appears that David's situation, for the moment at least, seemed hopeless without God's intervention. Psalm 91 provides the truths that bring the solution. The structure of Psalm 142 is as follows: (1) the cry of David (verses 1–2); (2) the circumstances of David (verses 3–4); and (3) the confidence of David (verses 5–7).

4. NO ONE. It appears to David that he has been totally abandoned.

5. YOU ARE MY REFUGE: A frequent claim in the psalms (see Psalms 7:1; 11:1; 16:1; 18:2; 25:20; 31:1; 46:1; 57:1; 61:3; 62:7; 91:2; 94:22; 141:8; 143:9; 144:2).

7. PRISON: The cave in which David was hidden.

APPEAL FOR GUIDANCE AND DELIVERANCE: No specific background is known for Psalm 143, which is the final penitential psalm (see Psalms 6; 32; 38; 51; 102; 130).

143:1. HEAR MY PRAYER: The structure of this psalm is as follows: (1) David's passion (verses 1–2); (2) David's predicament (verses 3–6); and (3) David's plea (verses 7–12).

FAITHFULNESS . . . RIGHTEOUSNESS: David appeals to God's character.

2. NO ONE LIVING IS RIGHTEOUS: David admits his own unrighteousness and realizes that if he is to be delivered for the sake of righteousness (see verse 11), it will be because of God's righteousness, not his own.

6. A THIRSTY LAND: As a drought-struck land yearns for life-giving water, so persecuted David longs for his life-giving deliverer.

7. YOUR FACE: An anthropomorphism picturing God's attention to the psalmist's plight.

10. YOUR SPIRIT: This refers to the Holy Spirit (see Psalms 51:11; 139:7).

11. YOUR NAME'S SAKE: David appeals to God's benefit and honor, not his own (see Psalms 23:3; 31:3; 79:9).

12. YOUR SERVANT: To attack God's servant is to attack God, thus bringing God to the rescue.

PRAISING GOD WHO PRESERVES AND PROSPERS HIS PEOPLE: Psalm 144, in part (verses 1–8), is very similar to Psalm 18:1–15. It could be that this psalm was written under the same kind of circumstances as the former, i.e., on the day the Lord delivered him from the hand of his enemies, including King Saul (see 2 Samuel 22:1–18).

144:1. BLESSED BE THE LORD: The structure is as follows: (1) God's greatness (verses 1–2); (2) man's insignificance (verses 3–4); (3) God's power (verses 5–8); (4) man's praise (verses 9–10); and (5) God's blessing (verses 11–15).

MY ROCK: David's foundation is God—solid and unshakeable (see Psalms 19:14; 31:3; 42:9; 62:2; 71:3; 89:26; 92:15; 95:1).

TRAINS MY HANDS FOR WAR: David lived in the days of Israel's theocracy, not the New Testament church (see John 18:36). God empowered the king to subdue His enemies.

2. LOVINGKINDNESS . . . REFUGE: God provided six benefits: (1) lovingkindness; (2) a fortress; (3) a high tower; (4) a deliverer; (5) a shield; and (6) a refuge.

3–4. WHAT IS MAN: Eternal God is contrasted with short-lived man (see Psalm 8:4).

5–8. BOW . . . TOUCH . . . FLASH . . . SHOOT: Highly figurative language is used to portray God as the heavenly warrior who comes to fight on behalf of David against God's enemies on earth.

9. A NEW SONG: A song of victory that celebrates deliverance/salvation (see Psalms 33:3; 40:3; 96:1; 98:1; 144:9; 149:1; Revelation 5:9; 14:3).

11. Rescue me: See verses 7–8.

12. SONS . . . DAUGHTERS: God's rescue of David's kingdom from foreigners would bring blessing on families.

13–14. BARNS . . . SHEEP . . . OXEN: Blessing would also come to the agricultural efforts.

14. NO BREAKING IN . . . GOING OUT . . . OUTCRY: Peace, not strife, would characterize the land.

> A SONG OF GOD'S MAJESTY AND LOVE: Psalm 145 represents
> David's exquisite conclusion to his seventy-three psalms in the
> Psalter. Here, he celebrates the King of eternity for who He is,
> what He has done, and what He has promised.

145:1. I WILL EXTOL YOU: Rich in content, this psalm also duplicates a majestic acrostic design by using the twenty-two letters of the Hebrew alphabet. Psalm 145 begins the great crescendo of praise that completes the Psalter and might be called "the Final Hallel" (Psalms 145–150). The structure of the psalm is as follows: (1) commitment to praise (verses 1–2); (2) God's awesome greatness (verses 3–7); (3) God's great grace (verses 8–13); (4) God's unfailing faithfulness (verses 14–16); (5) God's unblemished righteousness (verses 17–20); and (6) recommitment/exhortation to praise (verse 21).

MY GOD, O KING: David, king of Israel, recognized God as his sovereign (see Psalms 5:2; 84:3).

11–13. KINGDOM: David refers to the broadest use of kingdom in Scripture— i.e., God the eternal king ruling over all from before creation and eternally thereafter (see Psalm 10:16; Daniel 4:3; 7:27).

14–16. **THE LORD UPHOLDS ALL:** The emphasis is on God's common grace to all of humanity (see Matthew 5:45; Luke 6:35; Acts 14:17; 17:25).

20. **THE WICKED ... DESTROY:** The wicked await an eternity of living forever, away from the presence of God in the lake of fire (see 2 Thessalonians 1:9; Revelation 20:11–15).

UNLEASHING THE TEXT

1) How does Psalm 139 reflect the frailty and fragility of humankind?

_____

_____

_____

_____

2) How does Psalm 139 reflect the value and dignity of humankind?

_____

_____

_____

_____

3) Look specifically at Psalm 141:5. What does David mean when he expresses his desire for the righteous to "strike" and "rebuke" him?

_____

_____

_____

_____

4) What themes and images are reflected in David's final psalms (138–145)?

_____

_____

_____

_____

EXPLORING THE MEANING

There is no hiding from God. Psalm 139 is one of David's most famous poems, complete with powerful imagery and prose. The primary theme is God's deep knowledge of humanity in general and of David in particular. A cursory reading might give the impression that David was fearful or annoyed by God's constant attention: "O LORD, You have searched me and known me. You know my sitting down and my rising up; You understand my thought afar off" (verses 1–2). "You have hedged me behind and before, and laid Your hand upon me" (verse 5). "Where can I go from Your Spirit? Or where can I flee from Your presence?" (verse 7). But instead, David declared, "Such knowledge is too wonderful for me; it is high, I cannot attain it" (verse 6). Why was God's complete knowledge of David's life "wonderful"? Because David understood his flaws and imperfections. He understood his shortcomings and found comfort in God's complete sovereignty. Just as children play more freely at school when surrounded by a fence—when they have boundaries—so David took comfort in God's closeness.

God is intimately involved with His creation, including humanity. Not only does God have perfect knowledge about our thoughts and our actions, but He is also deeply involved in our creation. This is true in a general sense, in that God is the Creator of all things—everything that exists has come about because of His power and His will. Yet this is also true in a personal sense. God did not just create "humanity" as a mass collective. Rather, He has intricately hand-crafted each individual human being. "For You formed my inward parts," David wrote. "You covered me in my mother's womb. I will praise You, for I am fearfully and wonderfully made" (Psalm 139:13–14). Also, "My frame was not hidden from You, when I was made in secret, and skillfully wrought in the lowest parts of the earth" (verse 15). That included David, and it includes each of us. *Every* person has been fearfully and wonderfully made. *Every* person is a treasured masterpiece specially designed by the very hands of God.

We should recognize our need for God in every detail of our lives. In reviewing David's more introspective psalms, it is interesting to see how often he pleads for God to join him or support him in specific moments or with specific needs. Even though David was aware of God's sovereignty and authority—not to mention God's intimate knowledge of his life—David was intentional about requesting

God's presence and help. Psalm 141 is a great example. When David needed help controlling his tongue, he sought God: "Set a guard, O LORD, over my mouth; keep watch over the door of my lips" (verse 3). When David needed wise counsel from trusted advisors, he asked God to deliver it (verse 5). And when David needed protection from the schemes of evil men, he again invited God to provide it: "Keep me from the snares they have laid for me, and from the traps of the workers of iniquity. Let the wicked fall into their own nets, while I escape safely" (verses 9–10). These desperate cries for help represent David's deep knowledge of how God worked in his life.

REFLECTING ON THE TEXT

5) What might cause people to try and hide from God?

_____

_____

_____

_____

_____

6) What are some practical implications regarding God's complete and intimate knowledge of every detail of our lives?

_____

_____

_____

_____

_____

7) Why is it important to take time for introspection on a regular basis? Does that introspection lead to focusing upon God?

_____

_____

_____

_____

_____

8) Though David was in a unique relationship with God, how can you apply his thoughts and reflections?

_____

_____

_____

_____

_____

_____

PERSONAL RESPONSE

9) What sins are preventing you from examining your own heart in relation to God's standard of holiness?

_____

_____

_____

_____

_____

_____

10) What would it look like for you to see your need for God's constant provision in your life today? Right this moment?

_____

_____

_____

_____

_____

_____

12

REVIEWING KEY PRINCIPLES

DRAWING NEAR
Do the Psalms motivate you? Do they convict you?

_____

_____

_____

_____

_____

_____

_____

_____

_____

_____

_____

_____

_____

_____

THE CONTEXT
When teaching children about the structure of God's Word and the many different books present within the Scriptures, it is often noted that one can find the Psalms simply by opening to the middle of the Bible. While that is primarily a trick of modern page counts and binding methods, it is not a mistake to say

that worship is the core of God's Word. Praise is a critical foundation on which to build our spiritual lives.

In our journey through the Psalms, we have seen the power of actively worshiping God for His character and His great works. We have seen the beauty of meditating on who God is and what He has done. And we have seen the importance of crying out to God and seeking His favor even in the midst of terrible circumstances.

Below you will find a few of the major principles we have found during our study of Psalms. There are many more we do not have room to reiterate, so take some time to review the earlier studies—or better still, to meditate on the passages of Scripture we have covered. As you do, ask the Holy Spirit to give you wisdom and insight into His Word.

EXPLORING THE MEANING

Pursuing righteousness does not preclude individual aspirations. Submitting to the will of God does not necessarily mean that we give up personal desires. We should never pursue anything that is opposed to God and His righteous character, but we are free to enjoy whatever is not immoral. Nevertheless, we are called to submit everything we do to the will of God, seeking to honor Him in everything. If you "delight yourself also in the LORD," then "He shall give you the desires of your heart" (Psalm 37:4). But notice that "delight[ing] . . . in the LORD" is the condition He demands before you receive "the desires of your heart." This means that whatever you desire is in accordance with God's character, or at least not contrary to it. Therefore, you are free to pursue your own heart's desires so long as those desires do not violate God's law. Ecclesiastes 11:9 reads, "Rejoice, young man, during your childhood, and let your heart be pleasant during the days of young manhood. And follow the impulses of your heart and the desires of your eyes. Yet know that God will bring you to judgment for all these things" (NASB).

We can find comfort in God's Word. Psalm 19 begins with wonderful expressions of praise to God, with David connecting different aspects of creation to the glorious nature of God's character. The second half of the psalm shifts away from the world and focuses squarely on God's Word: "The law of the LORD is perfect, converting the soul; the testimony of the LORD is sure, making wise the simple;

the statutes of the LORD are right, rejoicing the heart; the commandment of the LORD is pure, enlightening the eyes" (verses 7–8). These are beautiful expressions of admiration and adoration from David for the Scriptures—both for what they themselves are, and for what they accomplish in our lives. The Bible is more desirable than gold, "Yea, than much fine gold," and, "Sweeter also than honey and the honeycomb" (verse 10). The incredible value of God's Word should not be lost on modern readers who, unlike David, have access to the full canon of Scripture. That value can be an amazing source of comfort. No matter what happens in life—no matter what we endure or what we might face—we have access to the very words of God spoken to bless and benefit us.

True repentance leads to forgiveness. Why should Christians repent of their sin? First, because sin disrupts our communion with God and is harmful in our lives. Second, because God actively desires to forgive His children and sanctify them. True and genuine repentance is the door we walk through in order to receive that forgiveness, and by God's grace, He convicts us to repent of our sin. Psalm 51 is David's public confession after his sinful choices with Bathsheba and Uriah. Notably, he began that repentance by acknowledging God's forgiving character: "Have mercy upon me, O God, according to Your lovingkindness; according to the multitude of Your tender mercies, blot out my transgressions" (verse 1). In Psalm 32, David offered a timeline of sorts regarding his confession, repentance, and forgiveness. His initial attempts to hide his sin caused a rift in his relationship with God and a growing burden within his heart. Then, David made the choice to repent (see verse 5), and that repentance led to God's forgiveness: "I said, 'I will confess my transgressions to the LORD,' and You forgave the iniquity of my sin" (verse 5).

Worship must be a priority for followers of God. The sons of Korah were likely vocal performers rather than the official authors of the eleven psalms that bear their name. But even the existence of a group like them should give us pause. In the midst of a vast and complex sacrificial system—with different groups of the Levitical tribe tasked with all manner of jobs—one group was given the specific assignment of singing God's praises and leading others to do the same. Why? Because worship is a priority! When we rightly understand who God is and who we are, worship should naturally overflow through our lives—and through our lips. As we've seen, David made worship a priority. From the time he was an unknown shepherd all the way through his most glorious accomplishment as king, David worshiped God and helped others express their worship to God. Similarly, in our journey of following Christ, we must always remember that worshiping God is more than singing a few songs every Sunday. Worship is the posture of our lives as we praise and appreciate our sovereign Lord.

God's blessings are insurmountable. Psalm 73 is an interesting study of the question that is also found in the book of Job: *Why do the wicked prosper?* The psalmist had evidently wrestled with that question for some time, and he started the song with his conclusion: "Truly God is good to Israel, to such as are pure in heart" (verse 1). After stating that principle, he looked back to his time of struggle. He confessed he "was envious of the boastful, when I saw the prosperity of the wicked" (verse 3). He wondered why the wicked of his day seemed to have such blessed lives in spite of their rebellion against God's will and God's values. He even wondered if he had chosen the wrong path. The turning point for the psalmist's contemplations was an encounter with God in the sanctuary, where he realized the blessings of the wicked were fleeting, but serving God offered value for eternity. This realization culminates in one of the loveliest expressions in all of Scripture: "Whom have I in heaven but You? And there is none upon earth that I desire besides You. My flesh and my heart fail; but God is the strength of my heart and my portion forever" (verses 25–26).

God alone is worthy of praise. In Psalm 89, Ethan contemplates what feels like a conundrum. God had chosen Israel as His covenant people and promised to bless David's descendants forever. Yet as Ethan looked at his world, he saw Israel divided and David's dynasty in tatters. How could he reconcile those two truths? As he wrestled with these ideas, Ethan began his contemplation on what he knew was solid ground: that God is sovereign and worthy of praise. Like Ethan, we will best deal with the issues of our day when we focus first on the wonder and glory of God and choose to praise Him. God alone is worthy of praise, and we receive strength and steadfastness when we ground ourselves in worship. Incidentally, Ethan never found a resolution in his psalm to his questions about God's sovereignty and the plight of Israel. He left the matter open for future resolution. However, with the benefit of history, we can see the answer to his question today, namely, Jesus Christ. Through Christ, therefore, God has partially fulfilled His promise to Israel and will one day restore them as a nation in the promised land.

Without God's compassion, we are lost. In many ways, Moses' prayer in Psalm 90 is a foreshadowing of the gospel. Specifically, Moses understood our inability to deal with our own sin. As Paul wrote in Romans 3:23, "For all have sinned and fall short of the glory of God." Because of this understanding, the final portions of Moses' prayer are laser-focused on God's mercy and compassion. "Have compassion on Your servants," he prayed. "Oh, satisfy us early with Your mercy, that we may rejoice and be glad all our days!" (verses 13–14). His concluding plea is both poignant and passionate: "And let the beauty of the LORD our God be upon us, and establish the work of our hands for us; yes, establish the work of our hands" (verse 17). Scripture makes it clear that we are helpless to solve the problem of our sin. We are dead in our trespasses, and the wages of our sin is death—both physically and spiritually. Like Moses, we must appeal to God's compassion for salvation. Yet the wonderful news of the gospel is that salvation has already been accomplished, and it is applied to those who believe it through repenting of their sin and placing their faith in Christ.

We should recognize our need for God in every detail of our lives. In reviewing David's more introspective psalms, it is interesting to note how often he pleads for God to join him or support him in specific moments or with specific needs. Even though David was aware of God's sovereignty and authority—not to mention God's intimate knowledge of his life—David was intentional about requesting God's presence and help. Psalm 141 is a great example. When David needed help controlling his tongue, he sought God: "Set a guard, O LORD, over my mouth; keep watch over the door of my lips" (verse 3). When David needed wise counsel from trusted advisors, he asked God to deliver it (verse 5). And when David needed protection from the schemes of evil men, he again invited God to provide it: "Keep me from the snares they have laid for me, and from the traps of the workers of iniquity. Let the wicked fall into their own nets, while I escape safely" (verses 9–10). These desperate cries for help represent David's deep knowledge of how God worked in his life.

UNLEASHING THE TEXT

1) What verses have encouraged you most in this study? Why?

_____

_____

_____

_____

_____

2) What verses challenged you most in this study? Why?

_____

_____

_____

_____

_____

3) How has studying the book of Psalms added to your understanding and love of Jesus?

_____

_____

_____

_____

_____

_____

4) Why is worship a critical foundation for the lives of Christ-followers?

_____

_____

_____

_____

_____

PERSONAL RESPONSE

5) Have you repented of your sin and placed your faith in the finished work of Jesus Christ? Do you strive to put off sin and put on righteousness out of love for Him? Explain.

_____

_____

_____

_____

_____

6) What sins have you been most convicted of during this study? What will you do to address these sins? What will that look like over time? Be specific.

_____

_____

_____

_____

7) What have you learned about God's nature and character throughout this study? How should that knowledge affect your everyday life?

_____

_____

_____

_____

_____

8) In what areas do you hope to grow spiritually over the coming weeks and months? What steps will you need to take in order to achieve that growth?

_____

_____

_____

_____

If you would like to continue in your study of the Old Testament, read the next title in this series: *1 Kings 1–11, Proverbs, and Ecclesiastes.*

Also Available in the
John MacArthur Bible Study Series

The MacArthur Bible Studies provide intriguing examinations of the whole of Scripture. Each of the 35 guides (16 Old Testament and 19 New Testament) incorporates extensive commentary, detailed observations on overriding themes, and probing questions to help you study the Word of God.

Available now at your favorite bookstore.
More volumes coming soon.

 Harper*Christian*
Resources

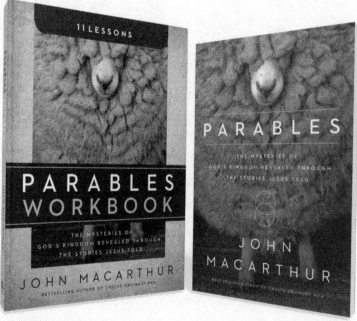